W9-AAK-349

An Urgent Call TO A Serious Faith

DAVE HUNT

HARVEST HOUSE PUBLISHERS
Eugene, Oregon 97402

Cover by Koechel Peterson & Associates, Minneapolis, Minnesota

AN URGENT CALL TO A SERIOUS FAITH
Copyright © 2000 by Dave Hunt
Published by Harvest House Publishers
Eugene, Oregon 97402

Library of Congress Cataloging-in-Publication Data

Hunt, Dave.
    An urgent call to a serious faith / Dave Hunt.
        p. cm.
    Includes bibliographical references.
    ISBN 0-7369-0313-5
    1. Christian life. I. Title.

    BV4501.2 .H8257 2000
    48.4—dc21   99-056888

Printed in the United States of America.

00 01 02 03 04 05 06 07 08 09 / BC / 10 9 8 7 6 5 4 3 2 1

CONTENTS

Part III: Living in the Gospel

Part IV: Deepening Our Faith

The author's free monthly newsletter
may be received by request. Write to:

Dave Hunt
PO Box 7019
Bend, OR 97708

or phone 800 937 6638

Part I

Why an Urgent Call?

1

The Necessity
of Certainty

*Teach us to number our days, that we may apply
our hearts unto wisdom.*
—PSALM 90:12

Death is not a pleasant topic, nor one which we will dwell upon, but it is an important starting point for serious reflection. Moses wrote, "So teach us to number our days [that is, to realize how quickly they come to an end], that we may apply our hearts unto wisdom" (Psalm 90:12). The implication is clear that something lies beyond the grave for which we ought to make plans. In full agreement, King David wrote, "LORD, make me to know mine end...the measure of my days...that I may know how frail I am" (Psalm 39:4). That

> The uncertainty of life and the inevitability of death are two of the most basic elements of human existence.

realization would only be depressing and much to be avoided unless there is something after death for which we should prepare. In the same vein, Solomon declared: "It is better to go to the house of mourning [that is, a funeral], than to go to the house of feasting: for that is the end of all men; and the living will lay it to his heart" (Ecclesiastes 7:2).

The uncertainty of life and the inevitability of death are two of the most basic elements of human existence. Logically, then, what may lie after death deserves at least some serious attention and planning before it may be forever too late. And it is only reasonable that prior to that awesome moment of death, which overtakes all in its own time and without discrimination, one needs to be absolutely certain what death will bring and exactly why.

Absolutely certain? Of course, because nothing less will do. Regardless of one's religious belief or lack of it, death puts its terminating stamp upon every earthly passion, position, possession, and ambition. There is a finality to death that shouts, "Too late! Too late!"

Inasmuch as death could come knocking at any time, regardless of one's age, health, or expectations, there is great urgency in knowing with absolute certainty what lies beyond death's door. No matter how young we may be or how healthy we may seem, that dread event draws steadily and inexorably closer for each one of us—and often comes as an unwelcome surprise.

Of Juliet, Lady Capulet mourned, "Death lies on her like an untimely frost upon the sweetest flower of the field." In *Paradise Lost* Milton expressed the universal horror that anyone could become "Food for so foul a Monster" as death. Homer's *Iliad*, written in the eighth-century B.C., lamented, "Death in ten thousand shapes hangs ever over our heads, and no man can elude him." That being the case, there is great urgency to know what lies before us when death releases us from these material bodies. There is no known recovery once one passes through death's door into whatever lies beyond.

The view that death's consequences ought to be a matter of grave concern is opposed by three alternative beliefs. Some insist there is nothing beyond death either to prepare for or to fear. Their mantra, which they desperately want to believe in order to be relieved of any thought of possible judgment, goes like this: "When you're dead, you're dead; that's it, period." Others, while believing in an afterlife, still manage to relieve themselves of any concern by subscribing to the theory that in the next life our spirits meet perfect acceptance no matter what we may have done in this life. We simply continue to learn further lessons as we progress ever upward. Still others are convinced that our souls migrate into new bodies, providing the opportunity to come back to earth to live again and again, hopefully to progress in each succeeding life.

We'll consider these three popular theories, the first one in this chapter and the other two in the next. The idea that death is the end of one's existence is founded upon materialism: the theory that nothing exists but matter. Therefore, there is no soul or spirit to survive the death of the body; nor do God, Satan, angels, devils, or anything else that isn't physical exist. This atheistic theory is appealing and many would like to believe it because there would be no future judgment to face for one's misdeeds. Such a belief can be easily dismissed, however, on the basis of much evidence to the contrary.

That we are each more than our physical bodies is evident from the fact that we hold ideas and thoughts which are not physical and therefore cannot be part of the physical brain. To the ancient assertion, "I think, therefore I am," must be added, "My thoughts are nonmaterial, therefore so am I." That being the case, where do these thoughts reside, what form do they take, and what is their origin? These questions, for which materialism has no answer, must be seriously and honestly faced.

There is no way that chemical reactions and electrical impulses among the brain's cells can explain a sense of right and wrong, the beauty of a sunset, or the rational and moral choices we continually make. No material of any kind, either in the brain or outside of it, has any qualities to explain our ability to understand ideas such as truth, justice, holiness, mercy, and grace. These concepts are totally nonphysical. They do not originate within the brain, nor are they a conditioned response to anything anywhere in the entire physical universe.

Indeed, the brain does not think at all. If thoughts originated in the brain, we would be prisoners of our brains, compelled to do whatever the brain decided. On the contrary, every person is convinced that he or she makes rational choices by weighing alternatives, not because the brain gets an impulse to make the body act in a certain way. While we are prone to react impulsively to the stimuli of physical temptations that breed lust, we are not forced to do so. The moral struggles we all experience to resist temptation are proof that we are not stimulus-response mechanisms ruled by impulses but that we do make genuine choices, though not always rational ones.

Without a doubt there is a "ghost in the machine," something nonphysical inhabiting the body. There must be a human spirit which thinks these nonphysical thoughts, which holds these concepts that have no source in the physical universe, and which makes rational and moral choices. The brain is like a computer which the spirit, the real person within, uses to operate the body in order to function on this physical plane and to interact with other souls and spirits who also occupy similar bodies.

A man complains bitterly, "There's no justice in this world!" What is he talking about? If it doesn't exist on earth, he has obviously never had any contact with that quality of justice which he is complaining ought to be here but isn't. Yet he knows it exists. Where could that be, and how does he know about it? How does he even have the concept of "justice" (or of grace, truth, holiness, and selfless love) if he is only the material of his body and has had no physical contact with justice by sight, hearing, taste, touch, or smell? Indeed, justice has none of these physical qualities but is unquestionably nonphysical.

Materialism simply won't hold up to examination. It cannot explain even the simplest realities of life as we daily experience it. Much less can materialism explain profound thoughts, philosophical concepts, the drive to expand one's knowledge, and the yearning for purpose and meaning even beyond this physical life. Undeniably, the appreciation of truth, wisdom, and beauty, the loathing of evil, and the longing for ultimate fulfillment do not arise from any quality of the atoms, molecules, or cells that comprise the body. There is therefore good reason to believe that the spirit to which these undeniably *spiritual* capacities belong will continue to exist even when the body it has inhabited dies.

There is no denying the fact that even though we have never seen it on earth, each of us innately recognizes a perfect standard of absolute justice, truth, and holiness. Moreover, we have something we call a "conscience" which tells us when we have violated that

> "We are mirrors whose only brightness, if we are bright at all, depends entirely upon the sun that shines upon us."
> —C.S. Lewis

standard. We can learn to turn a deaf ear to this inner voice or to pervert it, but it is there nevertheless. Once again, the conscience can only be explained on the basis that there is, residing in these physical bodies, a nonmaterial spirit created in the image of a personal God who is a Spirit and has impressed His standards upon us. And it can only be from Him that the obviously spiritual capabilities we possess derive.

The consciousness of having broken an unseen standard of right and wrong goes beyond culture and cannot be explained in terms of learned behavior. We can *reason* about what is right and wrong and decide upon behavior totally at odds with our upbringing and presumed conditioning. This fact is proved again and again as generation after generation rebels against the standards they have been taught. The hippies of recent interest are but one example.

Sin is coming short of that perfection for which God created us in order to reflect His own glory. As C.S. Lewis put it, "We are mirrors whose only brightness, if we are bright at all, depends entirely upon the sun that shines upon us." Sin is rejecting God's light, refusing to let it guide and energize us in God's will. We know when we have done that, and that sense of coming short is what troubles the conscience.

Conscience? Yes, we all have an inner recognition, which cannot be denied, of doing right or wrong. The man who complains about the injustice of a court decision need not be referring to a violation of any legislated law. In fact, far from accepting every law passed by legislative bodies, we often complain about *their* injustice. The man sitting in court and observing what he considers to be improper procedure and conclusion is really demanding that the court itself adhere to the innate standard which he knows exists and believes the court has violated.

In fact, the courts themselves have always drawn upon that standard. There is no written rule of conduct to cover every situation that might arise. One of the most famous cases decided by the Supreme Court of the United States involved two men and a boy drifting for days in a lifeboat. The men decided that it was better to kill the boy than for all three to die for lack of water and sustenance. Evidence produced in court demonstrated that had they not killed the boy all three indeed would have died. No legislative body had ever written a law to cover such a situation. Nonetheless, the court, drawing upon a higher source of right and wrong, found the two men guilty of murder.

No one has the right to take another's life to save oneself. That rule is written in our conscience. But it is the very opposite of everything that evolution, were it true, would produce as instinctive reaction. Self-preservation is the law of the jungle and enforced by tooth and claw without compassion. Respect for others is highly regarded among humans, and survival of the fittest could never produce it. Everywhere in nature, creatures kill and feed upon one another. We consider that normal and ourselves feed upon lower life forms which we have killed for our sustenance.

At the same time, however, we know it is wrong to kill other human beings of whatever color, race, or creed. The random motions of atoms in our brains that presumably all began with a big bang and have proceeded by chance ever since could not produce the moral understanding that binds us. Nor can moral conviction or compassion for others be explained by any evolutionary process. In fact, "survival of the fittest" would be undermined by conscience and ethical concerns.

Furthermore, in spite of "thou shalt not commit murder" being written indelibly in every conscience, man finds *reasons* to kill and even to torture his fellows. These rationalizations include supposedly justifiable wars, ethnic hatred, and religious fanaticism. Man has his devious explanations by which he can justify almost any evil. He is a *rational* being, even accusing others of being *irrational*, the worst insult one can level at another. But big bangs and chance motions of atoms do not produce rationality.

Reason is not a quality of matter but an ability of persons. Consequently, a person must consist of something more than the material of the body. Nor can a physical universe explain the existence of personal beings with the ability to reason about their origin. That could only come about through an infinite Being having created them in His image and likeness so that they could know and love Him and one another and receive His and others' love. That we recognize love as the highest experience and that the expression of human love involves not just the physical pleasure of an animal body, but something so far beyond it that it can only be described as spiritual, is further proof of man's true origin at the hand of God—and that he is more than the physical composition of his body.

The very fact that we have a conscience apart from culture, and an innate sense of justice that does not derive from man's laws but even complains about their injustices, can only be explained in one way: our spirits living in these bodies were created in the spiritual image of the God who is perfect in justice, holiness, love, truth, and those other nonphysical attributes which only God could possess in flawless fullness. This innate realization within is like an echo from a distant paradise of perfection we know must exist though we've never been there. And whenever these moments of insight are honestly faced we feel a haunting emptiness that seems to be saying that we were created for an excellence which was somehow lost to our race.

Even Lenin could not escape this realization. Boasting that communism was "scientific atheistic materialism," Lenin foolishly insisted that man was a physical stimulus-response organism and all he could know was through the stimulus of physical phenomena. Lenin was correct, however, in this: that we cannot even think of anything that doesn't exist. This is easily proved by the fact that we cannot imagine a new prime color for the rainbow. We can think of "pink elephants," but pink and elephants both exist. Even the extraterrestrials portrayed on the screen in the most fantastic science fiction and space odyssey movies are merely corruptions or bizarre combinations of creatures we know from earth experience.

Then how do we have the concept of God? If the only thought or understanding we can hold must be aroused by the stimulus of some physical object, what physical stimulus evokes the idea of God whom we understand to be the ultimate nonphysical Being? Obviously, there is no such physical stimulus. We could not possibly invent God. Then what was it that aroused the idea of God in the human mind, an idea beyond any physical thing we have ever observed?

Lenin couldn't answer that question without abandoning his atheism, which he refused to do in spite of the evidence for God's existence. The same holds true for Satan, angels, demons, and discarnate human spirits. The very fact that we have this concept of spirit beings and that it is not of this world is proof that some reality beyond the physical dimension has been able to establish itself in human consciousness. The evidence is overwhelming that the death of the physical body is not the end of human existence nor of human experience; it is the release of the human soul and spirit from the earthly connection to its physical body into a purely spiritual dimension.

Inasmuch as our existence continues after the death of the body, we dare not approach death without real certainty as to what lies beyond. Nor is there any time to waste. We don't have the option of deciding when we are ready to die. Death comes calling upon us when it will, and that could happen at any moment. Logically, the very fact that we are spirit beings temporarily living in bodies who may well exist eternally, demands great urgency in determining our future with absolute certainty.

How astonishing, then, that so few take death seriously enough to investigate thoroughly what lies beyond, and seem content to rely upon little more than their own casual opinion. Nor is it any less amazing that so many of those who do concern themselves with the question of what lies beyond death's door are willing to trust their eternal destiny to the word of a Joseph Smith, Mary Baker Eddy, eastern guru, priest, pope, pastor, psychological counselor, seminary or university professor. Only a fool would step out into eternity trusting his own or another's invented hopes.

2

Of God and Human Destiny

Before the mountains were brought forth,
or ever thou hadst formed the earth
and the world, even from everlasting
to everlasting, thou art God.
—Psalm 90:2

Eternity. What does it mean and why should one even embrace the concept, particularly with regard to human destiny? We know from personal experience and simple observation that material things wear out. The second law of thermodynamics tells us that the entire universe is wearing out, running down like a clock, and will not last indefinitely. Obviously then, it must have had a beginning, exactly as the Bible declares.

We know the sun has not been in the sky forever or it would have burned out by now. The same is true of all the other suns. Very clearly there was a time when this

> The intellect that designed the universe must be infinite and without beginning, a fact that points to God.

universe did not exist; nothing existed, not even the energy out of which the universe seems to be made. Why can't energy be postulated as without beginning? Because energy has neither the intellect nor personal qualities to bring about the incredible design in life and the existence of personal beings. These could not have arisen later out of energy or matter, so they must have preceded it. The intellect that designed the universe must be infinite and without beginning, a fact that points to God.

Intellect and personality, however, no matter how great, are not the stuff of which matter is made. Therefore, the universe is neither part of God nor an extension of God. This means that everything we can see, whether with the naked eye, with a telescope, or with an electron microscope, came from nothing. That is impossible, but we are driven to this conclusion by logic itself. To imagine, however, that life and intelligence sprang spontaneously of its own initiative and power from dead, empty space would be totally irrational. Therefore, something other than the universe and its components must have always existed.

No, not *something* but *Someone*, without beginning or end. Why *Someone?* Because the universe, from the structure of the atom to the human cell, exhibits order and a magnificent intricacy of design which only an infinite intelligence could have planned and put together—and no thing or force or "higher power" has the ability to think and plan and organize. Furthermore, the human race is composed of individual personalities who possess the ability to conceive conceptual ideas, express them in words or designs, and turn them into intricate structures foreign to nature. They have the ability, as well, to experience love and hate, joy and sorrow, justice and injustice, and to reason about their very existence and destiny.

Only an infinite Person could create persons. So we are driven by evidence and logic to conclude that this universe could have come into existence only at the command of Someone who had no beginning, Someone who always existed and innately possessed the infinite genius and power to bring everything and everyone into existence *out of nothing*. Of course, that One with neither beginning nor end is God. As Moses declared: "Before...ever thou hadst formed the earth...even from everlasting to everlasting, thou art God...a thousand years in thy sight are but as yesterday when it is past, and as a watch in the night" (Psalm 90:2,4).

This is not the god of paganism, of indigenous religions, or of any of the major world religions such as Buddhism (very few Buddhists believe in God), Hinduism, Islam, and others, but the God of the Bible who, as revealed therein, uniquely qualifies to be the Creator of all. For reasons that will become clear, we do not consider Christianity to be one of the world's religions, but distinct from all of them.

The Bible never tries to prove God's existence. It simply states it as a fact. Nor does the Bible attempt to explain what is beyond our ability to comprehend. It simply declares in its very first verse, "In the beginning God created the heaven and the earth" (Genesis 1:1). In gratitude to the God who had made him, David said, "I will praise thee; for I am fearfully and wonderfully *made*: marvelous are thy *works*; and that my soul knoweth right well" (Psalm 139:14).

Science has not been able, nor will it ever be able, either to verify, to refute, or to improve upon that declaration. We cannot understand it but are asked to accept it by faith. And here we have an example of what faith is: rather than an irrational leap, it is a rational step which follows the evidence and logic as far as reason is able, then takes another step beyond reason, always and only in the direction that evidence and reason have pointed.

The Bible puts it like this: "Through faith we understand that the worlds were framed by the word of God, so that things that are seen were not made of things which do appear" (Hebrews 11:3). Some have called this the first statement of the atomic theory. No, it is not theory; it is a statement of fact from God Himself. Be careful, however, not to read more into this verse than it actually says. It does not say that everything is made out of something invisible. It doesn't, in fact, say that the universe is made out of anything.

What Hebrews 11:3 tells us is that the visible universe was not made out of anything visible, for that would mean that something visible always existed and the universe was simply manufactured from materials at hand. On the contrary, that could not be the way it came about because nothing visible is eternal. In fact, the universe was created by the Word of God: "God said, Let there be..." (Genesis 1:3,6,9, and so on), and everything that is visible came into existence in obedience to His Word. That same Word which created all and holds all together will speak again and all that is visible in the old creation will dissolve back into nothing:

> But the heavens and the earth, which are now, by the same word [by which they were created] are kept in store, reserved unto fire against the day of judgment and perdition of ungodly men (2 Peter 3:7).

Long before the second law of thermodynamics had been discovered, Jesus put it very clearly: "Heaven and earth shall pass away" (Matthew 24:35). The universe, however, is not destined to simply wear out due to the passage of untold billions of years. Under the inspiration of the Holy Spirit, Peter explained that all life on earth as we have known it will be summarily terminated, and the entire universe will be destroyed by God in judgment of man's and Satan's rebellion. In its place a new universe will be created:

> [On] the day of judgment...the heavens shall pass away with a great noise, and the elements shall melt with fervent heat, the earth also and the works that are therein shall be burned up...the heavens being on fire shall be dissolved....

> Nevertheless we, according to his promise, look
> for new heavens and a new earth, wherein
> dwelleth righteousness (2 Peter 3:7-13).

The word "heavens" is used in two ways in Scripture: for all that is physical in dimensional space beyond earth; and for the nonphysical abode of God, called by Jesus "my Father's house... [of] many mansions" (John 14:2). One is visible and temporal, while the other is invisible and eternal. This visible temporary universe is not all that exists. There is another dimension of existence that is neither physical nor visible— and it doesn't wear out or grow old with the passage of time, nor can it be destroyed, nor will it ever cease to exist.

Our bodies are visible and thus temporal, but our souls and spirits are invisible and thus eternal. When comparing the short life expectancy on earth to eternity, the only rational choice one can make is to be far more diligent in preparing for the latter than for the former. Therefore, the Bible urges us to give priority to eternity over time. Jesus put it like this:

> Lay not up for yourselves treasures upon earth,
> where moth and rust doth corrupt, and where
> thieves break through and steal: but lay up for
> yourselves treasures in heaven, where neither
> moth nor rust doth corrupt, and where thieves do
> not break through and steal (Matthew 6:19,20).

The temporal treasures of earth are composed of visible things; the eternal treasures in heaven are not visible to our physical eyes. Treasures we lay up on this earth must all be left behind when we leave earth for what lies beyond death's door. The great hope of the Christian is not to amass wealth in this life but to receive an eternal reward in heaven. Peter described that reward as an "inheritance incorruptible, and undefiled, and that fadeth not away, reserved in heaven for you, who are kept by the power of God through faith unto salvation ready to be revealed in the last time" (1 Peter 1:4,5). In the resurrection, these bodies of decaying flesh are exchanged for new "spiritual bodies" (1 Corinthians 15:44) which are both visible and invisible, physical and spiritual, "eternal in the heavens" (2 Corinthians 5:1).

Paul encouraged Christians to believe, in the midst of persecution and martyrdom, that "our light affliction [suffered in this life on earth], which is but for a moment, worketh for us a far more exceeding and eternal weight of glory; while we look not at the things which are seen, but at the things which are not seen: for the things which are seen are temporal; but the things which are not seen are eternal" (2 Corinthians 4:17,18). No one can either refute or improve upon that statement.

Everything we can now see is temporary. None of it will last forever, but our invisible souls and spirits will. Therefore, we must make our choices and plans in this life in preparation for the next, recognizing that our visible bodies are only temporary housing for our invisible souls and spirits. These latter are indestructible and will continue to exist after the body dies and is finally dissolved in the grave. Thus, the most solemn question anyone can face is this: "Where will you spend eternity?"

Materialists such as Lenin and Freud and their modern followers attempt to deny all of this. Hardcore materialists, however, are becoming a vanishing breed in face of the mounting evidence uncovered in scientific laboratories around the world for the existence of intelligent beings who have no bodies and yet are interacting with the human race. We document that evidence in detail in two books, *The New Spirituality* and *Occult Invasion*, so we will not duplicate it here.

Indeed, so strong is the evidence for the existence of such entities that many scientists who believe in the false and mathematically impossible theory of evolution (many top scientists recognize it as a fraud) are even suggesting that spirit beings could be the highest form of evolution. This is, for example, the opinion of Robert Jastrow, one of the world's leading astronomers, who identifies himself as an agnostic. The founder and for many years director of the Goddard Institute for Space Studies (which played a key role in the Pioneer, Voyager, and Galileo space probes), Jastrow has suggested:

> Life that is a billion years beyond us may be far beyond the flesh-and-blood form that we would recognize. It may be...disembodied and has escaped its mortal flesh to become something that old-fashioned people would call spirits....Maybe it can materialize and then dematerialize. I'm sure it has magical powers by our standards....

With all due respect to Jastrow, intelligence is not a quality of matter and therefore could not evolve even if evolution were a scientific fact. Bodies do not evolve into spirits. Yet what a perfect setup this theory provides for demons. What more could they ask than to have materialistic scientists attempting to contact extraterrestrial life out in space, which they are willing to accept as nonphysical beings that "old-fashioned people would call spirits..."! What would today's scientists call these entities and how could they be certain of either their identity or their intentions toward mankind? The methods, machines, and theories of materialistic science cannot deal with nonphysical entities, no matter what one wants to call them.

> We are spirit, soul, and mind in His image.

Nor could the existence of the human mind ever be explained by evolution. Far from evolving into a nonphysical form, intelligent life can *only be* nonphysical, for that is the nature of intelligence. In contrast to the brain, which is a physical organ, the mind, which uses the brain like a computer, is nonphysical. Reiterated here again, human intelligence can only be explained as a creation of God in His image and thus with similar capabilities of thought and choice and love, but on a finite human level. We are not physically in God's image because God, as Jesus said, "is a Spirit" (John 4:24). Rather, we are spirit, soul, and mind in His image.

That nonphysical and nonhuman intelligences exist and are communicating with mankind has been the conviction and experience of primitive peoples since the beginning of time. Through the use of the "sacred mushroom," or peyote or other psychoactive plants, indigenous peoples have always made contact with spirit beings as part of their pagan religious rituals. The use of psychedelic drugs within the last 45 years sparked a revival of paganism in the Western world. Through drugs, multitudes of westerners were initiated into another dimension inhabited by spirit entities and to the occult and Eastern philosophy which they consistently teach.

The phenomenon known as "channeling," whereby nonmaterial intelligences speak through human instruments, has been verified to be genuine (though there are phonies involved as well). One verification is in the fact that the messages that come independently through thousands of different channelers around the world (there are more than 1,000 in Los Angeles alone), in spite of no contact and no exchange of notes with one another, have an undeniable commonality that can only be explained as coming from a common nonhuman source.

Terrence McKenna, who has taken Timothy Leary's place as the foremost champion of drugs for the purpose of supposedly "raising consciousness," has traveled the world sampling psychoactive plants of all kinds and documenting their effects. He discovered that all of these substances were able to open contact to nonphysical entities who, says McKenna, "are trying to teach us something." Indeed, that appears to be their insidious purpose.

Moreover, the philosophy they communicate conforms precisely to the four lies with which the Bible says the serpent (Satan) deceived Eve in the Garden of Eden: 1) God is not personal but a Force; 2) there is no death; we don't die but survive in the spirit world (or get recycled in reincarnation); 3) we are evolving into gods; and 4) that process can be accelerated through initiation into secret knowledge with a dark and light side. There is no explaining away as mere coincidence this common message or its conformity to what the serpent taught Eve. On the contrary, it provides absolute proof of both the reality of such spirit communications and their true identity as demonic messengers of Satan indoctrinating mankind with what the Bible calls "doctrines of devils."

The New Testament comes down severely against something it calls "sorcery." The Greek word from which the English is translated is *pharmakeia* from which, of course, we get our word for pharmacy or drugs. We are told in the Bible that this practice of contacting the spirit world through drugs will permeate civilization in the last days. The world will refuse to repent of it and as a result God's judgment will fall: "neither repented they of...their sorceries...for by thy sorceries were all nations deceived...for without [excluded from heaven] are sorcerers..." (Revelation 9:21; 18:23; 22:15). Paul warned:

> Now the Spirit [of God] speaketh expressly, that in the latter times some shall depart from the faith, giving heed to seducing spirits, and doctrines of devils; speaking lies in hypocrisy; having their conscience seared with a hot iron...(1 Timothy 4:1,2).

Among the "doctrines of devils" these seducing spirits teach are the other two theories propounded to escape God's judgment after death. We mentioned them briefly in the first chapter. Let us consider first of all what is commonly called "spirit survival." Some of these communicating entities claim to be the spirits of persons who once lived on earth and died centuries or even thousands of years ago. They offer as "proof" bits of information known only to the dead person and the living relative or friend to whom the "spirit" now speaks through a medium. Of course, that does not provide foolproof identification of the "spirit" as being that of the deceased. On the contrary, we know these are "demons" impersonating deceased persons because they promote Satan's basic lies given to Eve in the Garden. Specifically, spirit survival comes from Satan's assertion, "Ye shall not surely die" (Genesis 3:4).

No wonder, then, that the Bible repeatedly forbids any attempt to communicate with the dead (Leviticus 20:6; Deuteronomy 18:9-12). Their spirits are either in heaven or hell, not flitting about on the so-called astral plane and able to communicate with those still alive on earth. Necromancy is, in fact, trafficking with demons, the very "seducing spirits" of which the Holy Spirit warns us through Paul.

Nevertheless, some of the information passed on is extremely convincing and the lies are irresistibly appealing. Who wouldn't want to believe there is neither death nor judgment and that we all have within us at our disposal infinite god-like powers if we only knew how to tap into them— a technique which these entities promote? Consequently, spiritism has had a great many followers since the beginning of time. Even today, this satanic delusion has hundreds of millions of adherents worldwide. It has always been and still is the prevailing religious belief among indigenous peoples everywhere on earth.

Claiming to have survived death, these seducing spirits allege that after leaving their physical bodies they faced no judgment but were accepted unconditionally by some higher being or white light regardless of what they had done in their life on earth. They further allege that after death one continues to live in a spirit world where one learns further lessons and progresses ever higher. From such communications the belief in "spirit survival" has arisen. Not only indigenous peoples, but many top leaders of the greatest nations in history (and in our modern world as well), such as Queen Victoria and Abraham Lincoln, have been devout believers.

A major problem with this theory is that it includes no accountability or punishment for past deeds. A Hitler presumably fares no worse than a Mother Teresa, except that it will take him longer to realize his alleged true potential. This version of "life after death," in effect, offers an escape through death from the very justice which our courts otherwise would have meted out on earth and which mankind's sense of right and wrong knows should be imposed by the ultimate Judge. That spiritism allows and condones this escape is an offense to the innate sense of justice we all possess.

Moreover, there is no evidence that anyone will "progress" in the spirit world. Why should one's behavior improve there from what it was here, especially in the absence of the motivation that might be supplied if there were serious consequences for evil? Spirit survival must be rejected because it goes against our innate concept of perfect justice and because there is absolutely no verifiable evidence to support it.

Closely related to spirit survival is a belief in reincarnation, also called transmigration of souls, another one of the "doctrines of devils" which the "seducing spirits" persuasively teach. Devotees reject the biblical teaching that "it is appointed unto men once to die, but after this the judgment" (Hebrews 9:27). Instead, there are allegedly many deaths and rebirths, because after death one's spirit enters the body of a newborn baby to live another life and die again—and another after that and yet another, and so on until one has progressed enough to escape the need to return again to earth's physical plane.

The Dalai Lama, for example, claims to be the 14th reincarnation of the original Dalai Lama of Tibet. Is there any proof? Only that he was born in Tibet very close to the time of death of the alleged 13th Dalai Lama. Nevertheless, this outrageous claim is accepted and he is hailed as a leading ambassador for world peace and religious unity. And how does he propose to bring peace to the world? Wherever he travels, the Dalai Lama initiates multitudes into Tibetan Tantric Deity Yoga, promising thereby (as the serpent promised Eve) to make them into gods who can create their own universe. For that he was given the Nobel Peace Prize! The world takes him so seriously that wherever he goes he is celebrated and received by dignitaries and heads of state.

In contrast to spirit survival, reincarnation includes the concept of punishment in the next life, imposed by something called "the law of Karma." The judgment it imposes, however, is without mercy and offers neither solution nor hope. In fact, Karma produces more evil in the process of supposedly punishing it. Reincarnation is thus amoral and can be dismissed on that basis alone, as well as because it is also senseless and hopeless.

Let us consider its amorality first. The horrible truth is that, rather than offering a solution to evil, it perpetuates evil. Karma and reincarnation work according to the alleged "law of cause and effect." Yes, the Bible, too, says, "whatsoever a man soweth, that shall he also reap" (Galatians 6:7). But that phrase is preceded by the words "God is not mocked," indicating that it is man's Creator—not an impersonal force—who causes him to reap what he sows.

Furthermore, according to the Bible, the "reaping" of the consequences of past deeds is not fatalistic as it is in reincarnation, but can be escaped by God's grace and forgiveness. The God of the Bible loves the sinner and has provided pardon from punishment, and He has done so on a righteous and judicially just basis. Instead of leaving man to suffer under an impersonal law of Karma, God loves us so much that He came as a man, through the virgin birth, to where we were in order to share in the trials of this life and to pay the penalty demanded by His own infinite justice for our rebellion. The Bible, therefore, is able to offer redemption and forgiveness of all sins to all who will receive God's gracious pardon on His terms, something reincarnation does not and cannot do.

According to the law of Karma, however, a man who beats his wife in this life must return in the next life as a wife beaten by her husband. There is no escape from this sentence. Thus, a thief or murderer must become the victim of the same crime. That the perpetrator of each crime must become the victim of the same crime means there must be another perpetrator, who must become the victim of yet another perpetrator, *ad infinitum, ad absurdum*. Instead of solving the problem of evil, reincarnation perpetuates it and is therefore amoral.

Reincarnation is also senseless. Who remembers the details of mistakes made and costly lessons learned in prior lives? No one. Then what is the point of coming back to life on earth again and again if one has no way of knowing whether lessons have been learned and progress is being made? Moreover, the increasing evil on earth proves that progress is not being made. The very concept of reincarnation is therefore senseless.

It is also hopeless. Supposedly the "bad karma" (whatever that means) which we build up in this life requires another life to "work it off." But in that very process we build up more bad karma, which requires yet another life, then another life, and so on endlessly. This is why the Hindu refers to "the wheel of reincarnation" (it just keeps rolling on endlessly) and Gandhi called it "a burden too great to bear."

What is happening to us in this life is presumably due to the karma of a prior life; but that was due to the karma of yet a prior life and so forth forever into the past. Going back through endless numbers of prior lives, one finally reaches the point when the three *gunas* of "God" were in perfect balance in the void. Inexplicably, something unknown caused an imbalance. As a result, the *prakriti* (manifestation) began and here we are, reaping the results of bad karma which began in "God", is locked into the very fabric of the universe, and can never be escaped! Reincarnation, therefore, is hopeless.

There is not a shred of evidence to support reincarnation. It is rather a lie of the serpent to prevent mankind from facing the reality of God's righteous judgment and accepting the forgiveness He offers. The few examples of people here and there who seem to have a fragmentary memory from a prior existence break down upon closer examination; and even those alleged memories are insufficient to form the basis for progress in their own lives, let alone for the entire human race. Being amoral, senseless, and hopeless and lacking any substantive evidence to support it, reincarnation must be rejected.

We are eternal beings who will spend eternity somewhere. Where will it be? And how can we know? There is no more important question to be faced and answered.

3

In Search of a Serious Faith

*But to him that worketh not, but believeth
on him that justifieth the ungodly, his faith is
counted for righteousness.*
—ROMANS 4:5

It is astonishing how many millions of otherwise seemingly intelligent people are willing to risk their eternal destiny upon less evidence than they would require for buying a refrigerator or a TV. Thomas Hobbes, for example, a seventeenth-century philosopher and mathematician who spent years analyzing the evil in man and attempting to find a social system to bring universal peace, failed to make adequate investigation and preparation for the next life. Consequently, as death approached, he made this sad confession, "Now I am about to take my last voyage, a great leap in the dark." It seems irrational to take a leap into the dark in any direction—but into *eternity*?

Omar Khayyam viewed death as the door of darkness to "the road which to discover we must travel too." But it's too late once one has passed through that "door" onto that unknown road. Thus Shakespeare suggested that "in that sleep of death what dreams may come when we have shuffled off this mortal coil, must give us pause...." But more than "pause" to reflect, we need certainty and we need it now, backed not by wishful thinking but by solid evidence.

Whatever expectations people entertain of life after death, such beliefs are generally categorized as part of their religion. Another word for religion is "faith," and by that definition there are many "faiths" in the world. "People of faith" (a term used for those who hold to some religious belief) are joining together in political and social action supposedly to make a better world. This cooperation to improve society for mutual benefit has brought a new tolerance for all religions, no matter how contradictory their opposing views. And here we face another anomaly: according to recent polls, a surprisingly high percentage (the majority among both Catholics and Protestants) of those who identify themselves with a particular religion nevertheless believe that many other religions, if not all, will also take their followers to whatever they call their "heaven."

> There is nothing more important than having a solid factual and rational basis for one's faith.

Religion is called faith because it is something one is generally expected to believe regardless of proof. Ask most religious people why they believe what they believe, and they would be at a loss to explain. More than likely their response would be to say loyally (for some, stubbornly) something like, "I was born a Baptist, and I'll die a Baptist"; or, "I was born a Catholic and I'll die a Catholic," or Methodist, Hindu, Buddhist, Muslim, atheist. Yet very few can give a solid reason why they believe what they believe (or don't believe), and many are offended when asked for one.

Right here we find something very odd. As noted above, most people are less careful when it comes to eternity than they are about buying a car or checking the labels for exact ingredients of foodstuffs, or for almost anything else in this life. That is evident from the weak reasons which are usually offered by those who attempt to justify their religious faith: "I like the pastor"; or, "The choir is fantastic"; or, "The people are so friendly"; or, "It's the closest church"; or, "They have a wonderful youth program"; or, "Our family has always belonged to this denomination"; or, "Some missionaries came to the door and invited us to attend and we weren't going anywhere, so...." It is incomprehensible that so few people really get serious about faith.

Yet there is nothing more important than having a solid factual and rational basis for one's faith. To the many who think of faith as a belief strongly held and without evidence to support it (and often even in spite of much evidence to the contrary), that may seem an outrageous statement. Logically, however, if believing something strongly doesn't make it so, as human experience daily proves, then it is the greatest folly to continue on with a "faith" which, because it has no basis in fact but merely in fancy, must inevitably prove to be empty. The cost could be eternal and irrecoverable.

That being the case, how much better it is to "lose" one's faith now while there is still time to discover the truth, than to find out too late that one has been following or living a lie. Such disillusionment often follows when a young person matures, leaves home to work or attend university or enter the armed services, and is no longer under parental and church influence. This could be the case whether one was a Buddhist, Hindu, Muslim, or an adherent of any other religion. The same holds true for someone who has claimed to be a Christian but doesn't really know the Lord.

Many a young person raised in a Christian home, having professed faith in Christ, and having long attended and even been active in a good evangelical church, has later rejected Christ on the basis of peer pressure or a little "higher education" or out of necessity to justify a godless lifestyle. This turning away from one's professed faith is often justified with the claim that there is no truth but that we have all, no matter what the religion, simply been conditioned to believe what we believe. Since the days of Freud, psychology has long propounded the theory that any religious faith is merely a conditioned response learned especially in youth. That may well be true in many cases, but it cannot serve as justification for abandoning what one has been taught from childhood. The issue is whether what one was persuaded to believe is the truth or not. Tragically, the truth has often been abandoned for a more appealing lie.

In fact, this idea of conditioning is a myth which must be dispensed with in our search for true faith. The very fact that the person has rebelled against his upbringing and alleged conditioning is itself proof that this theory is false. That multitudes of formerly religious persons offer what they consider to be *sound reason* for rejecting what they have been taught and once believed proves that the so-called conditioning upon which this theory rests didn't work, at least not in their case. The very rebellion the theory has been adopted to excuse disproves the conditioning theory.

Darwin faced a similar problem which still haunts evolutionists to this day. If we are simply the product of chance motions of atoms, beginning with an inexplicable explosion (of an unknown energy source) called "the big bang," then all of our thoughts are simply the result of chance motions of atoms in our brains and are thus without meaning—and that includes the theory of evolution itself. Whatever is going on in our brain cells at any moment must be traced back to that huge explosion, following which lifeless matter somehow came to life and over eons of time eventually evolved into human brain cells. There is no point in this process at which meaning could have been introduced, nor is there any rational source within matter or energy (they are interchangeable) from which a purposeful plan could have come.

Science can tell neither *where* the energy came from that was involved in the big bang nor *why* the explosion occurred. Indeed, if all we have to deal with is exploding energy, then to ask why (which implies meaning) is useless. There is no *why* or *wherefore* in energy and explosions. Shut down all universities and sit in mourning: there is no truth, no purpose, no meaning. Nor would we mourn at all for missing truth and meaning if we were merely the product of an explosion of energy, for such concepts would never result from random motions of atoms in our brains.

It is undeniable that there is neither truth, meaning, nor purpose without an intelligent Creator who, for His own reasons, made the universe and each of us in His image. Yet the world of academia largely rejects this inescapable fact. Professors and students claim to be on a quest for truth while denying that it exists or that anyone could identify it if it did. Such is the nihilistic atmosphere in major universities around the world. It is considered to be too dogmatic for anyone to claim that truth can be known. Then what is the point of research and study if all we can achieve is a listing of differing opinions, none of which can be declared to be either right or wrong?

This attitude has even found its way into theological seminaries and has spilled over from there into the thinking of most religious people. It is now considered presumptive or triumphalistic to suggest that there is only one true faith and that all others are wrong. That would be inexcusably offensive to those of other beliefs. As a result, when seeking to impress upon the average person the necessity of knowing for certain that one is following the right spiritual path into eternity, one hears repeatedly the popular refrain delivered with a shrug of the shoulders, "Aren't we all taking different roads to get to the same place?"

Although that sounds sufficiently broad-minded to avoid offending anyone, it is actually the ultimate in narrow-mindedness. While it allows everyone to take *different roads*, it insists that they must all end up in the *same place*. According to this dictum, there is only one destination beyond the grave. Once again, in violation of the sense of justice and fairness we all innately possess, a Hitler fares no worse than a Mother

Teresa. And those who suggest the contrary quickly find that this broad-minded tolerance is intolerant of any opinion that disagrees with it.

In an ancient form of this modern delusion, the Persian scriptures declare, "Whatever road I take joins the highway that leads to Thee....Broad is the carpet God has spread...." Jesus, too, spoke of a broad road that sounds very much like this "all roads" and "broad carpet"concept. However, far from commending it, He said it leads to destruction: "broad is the way that leadeth to destruction, and many there be which go in thereat: because strait is the gate, and narrow is the way which leadeth unto life, and few there be that find it" (Matthew 7:13,14). Jesus was not so dogmatic and narrow-minded as to say there is only one destination for all; He said there are two—heaven and hell. No one will be forced to go to either. Which of the two roads one takes is a matter of individual choice. Of course, if we choose to take the narrow road to God, it must be on His terms.

In an interesting essay in *Time* magazine (June 15, 1998), its author related an experience which illustrates the foolishness of today's unwillingness to take a definite stand when it comes to religious belief:

> As I checked in for a test at a local hospital the admissions lady inquired, "What is your religious preference?" I was tempted to repeat what Jonah said, "I am a Hebrew, ma'am. And I fear the Lord, the God of Heaven...." But that would have got me sent to psychiatry rather than x-ray....
>
> In ancient times, they asked, "Who is your God?" A generation ago, they asked your religion. Today your creed is a preference. According to Chesterton, tolerance is the virtue of people who do not believe in anything.
>
> When it is believed that on your religion hangs the fate of your immortal soul, the Inquisition follows easily; when it is believed that religion is a

breezy consumer preference, religious tolerance flourishes. After all, we don't persecute people for their taste in cars. Why for their taste in gods?

Oddly, though...there is one form of religious intolerance that does survive...the disdain bordering on contempt for those for whom religion is not a preference but a conviction....

A conviction that there is a definite way to heaven is not tolerated in this day of professed tolerance because it assumes that all roads *don't* lead to the same place, that truth *does* exist, and that there *is* a distinction between what is right and what is wrong. Instead of such old-fashioned convictions, ecumenical broad-mindedness is the new wave for the new millennium. We are expected to set aside the rational necessity of being certain about our eternal destiny in favor of a mindless tolerance that promises only to avoid religious arguments in this life but offers no sensible assurance for the next.

Tolerance sounds like a virtue, and at times it may be. On the other hand, an attitude allowing a parent to be tolerant of behavior that is harming a child or the police to be tolerant of criminals who prey upon others turns virtue into the vice of aiding and abetting evil. And to be tolerant of a false hope which has deceived multitudes and will lead them to destruction can hardly be the stance of one who truly loves others. This is why Paul said, "Knowing therefore the terror of the Lord, we persuade men..." (2 Corinthians 5:11).

The issue of where one will spend eternity is not a matter of preference, like joining the Elks instead of the Lions. Our opinions and inclinations cannot overturn what God has decreed. Why should the Creator tolerate and admit into His heaven rebels who have broken His laws, trampled on His Word, and rejected the salvation He offers? To imagine that is to credit God with the kind of indulgence of His creatures that we would condemn in a judge in an earthly court of law.

In his landmark book, *The Closing of the American Mind,* Chicago philosophy professor Alan Bloom pointed out that the one virtue in America these days seems to be openness to anything and everything as equally valid behaviors or points of view. Any and every opinion is greeted with equal tolerance—not conviction, but tolerance. It would be unacceptable dogmatism in most circles today to say that truth exists. That would mean that those who did not accept it would be wrong—and no one must be wrong.

Dr. Bloom points out that we have become so open to everything that our minds have been closed to the idea that something may indeed be true and something else false. The closing of the American mind through openness! That is exactly what is happening in the post-rational era which has overtaken our universities and seminaries and the thinking of many church leaders.

Again, simple logic would refute this idea of all roads leading to the same place. If words have any meaning, then we must acknowledge that there are serious contradictions between various world religions. They don't even agree upon the number of gods (millions for Hindus, one for Muslims, none for Buddhists), much less upon their identity or nature. Nor do world religions agree upon how to appease their god or gods or how to reach their version of heaven after death.

Jesus claimed that He is the only way to heaven: "I am the way, the truth, and the life: no man cometh to the Father, but by me" (John 14:6). He went so far as to say, "All that ever came before me are thieves and robbers" (John 10:8) and that includes Buddha, Confucius, and so on. Christianity stands not only in contrast but in opposition to all of the ways to heaven offered by the world's religions. Christ says they all lead to destruction. Surely His claims deserve careful investigation.

Without taking time to explain the many disagreements, it is undeniable that there are basic differences so great between the world's religions that it seems irrational to suggest that everyone is heading for the same place. Surprisingly, however, in spite of these differences, there is evidence that those who follow world religions will indeed all end up in the same place. Interestingly, we find in the world's various religious systems the same teachings that comprise the communications (doctrines of devils) to which we have earlier referred as coming from the spirit world. All religions have in common a universal opposition to the God of the Bible and His gospel concerning salvation by grace and faith alone—a commonality that places them all on one side and Christianity on the other.

Indeed, so wide is the chasm between Christianity and all the world's religions, that it seems equally clear that Christians will definitely arrive at a different eternal destiny from all the others. Yes, the various religions differ in the details relevant to the appeasement of their particular god or gods and the methods of attaining to nirvana or moksha or paradise. However, they all have in common the belief that their religious goals can somehow be achieved through their own efforts and/or faithful participation in rituals and sacraments. Whether by yoga or paying off bad karma for the Hindu, or by good deeds for the Muslim (or dying in Jihad [holy war] or on the Haj pilgrimage to Mecca), or through appeasing the spirits in African tribal religions and Shintoism, or by meditation techniques to escape desire and return to the void for the Buddhist, or by the sacraments of a supposed Christian church—it is all a matter of self-effort, which the God of the Bible firmly tells us He will not accept.

The Bible clearly states: "But to him that worketh not, but believeth on him that justifieth the ungodly, his faith is counted for righteousness" (Romans 4:5). Jesus said, "I came not to call the righteous, but sinners to repentance" (Mark 2:17). Paul emphasized that point: "Christ Jesus came into the world to save sinners" (1 Timothy 1:15). The world's religions, along with the false Christianity that employs sacramentalism, attempt to make a person righteous enough for heaven. In contrast, the Bible says that one must be a sinner, admit it, and believe the gospel to qualify for heaven.

Biblical salvation is by faith, and faith necessarily involves that which is unseen. It is not faith to believe in that which is present in visible form. Faith reaches out to the unseen world of the spirit and the eternal. And right here we encounter a major problem with ritual and sacraments: they attempt to rescue the unseen and nonphysical spirit and soul of man with physical and visible ceremony. It won't work.

> Biblical salvation is by faith, and faith necessarily involves that which is unseen.

This grave error of sacramentalism persists even among a majority of those who call themselves Christians. They imagine that through participation in the visible, and thus temporal, sacrament they receive invisible and eternal spiritual benefits. Clearly, this is impossible. The Bible declares, "Faith is the substance of things hoped for, the evidence of things not seen" (Hebrews 11:1). Salvation, because it is by faith, necessarily involves the eternal and invisible, not that which is seen and is therefore temporal.

Furthermore, ritual and sacraments have nothing to do with either justice or punishment and therefore cannot possibly pay for sin. One might as well imagine that some ritual could satisfy a court of law in paying the penalty prescribed for a major crime as imagine that God would accept sacraments in payment of the infinite penalty He has prescribed.

The Bible gives two sacraments for the Christian: baptism and communion (also called the Lord's supper). Both are symbolic reminders of a spiritual and eternal transaction that has already taken place: Christ's death for our sins and our identification with Him by faith in that great event. Neither baptism nor communion is efficacious, and to imagine that they are and therefore to rely upon either or both of them to effect even partially one's salvation is to reject the salvation God offers in grace to those who believe His promise.

In none of the world's religions is there any concept of God's perfect justice having to be satisfied for the sinner to be forgiven. Instead, works and rituals and mystical experiences are offered to appease God and/or to earn one's salvation. The Bible, however, finds all the world guilty of sin before God and insists that human guilt can only be forgiven on a righteous basis. The penalty that God decreed must be paid in full.

This attempt to offer works or rituals in payment of salvation is true even of some groups which claim to be Christian, but set up their own rules for salvation in opposition to the biblical gospel of salvation by faith and grace alone *without works*. The Bible clearly says: "...that whosoever believeth in him [Christ] should not perish, but have everlasting life" (John 3:16); "For by grace are ye saved through faith...not of works, lest any man should boast" (Ephesians 2:8,9); and "Not by works of righteousness which we have done, but according to his mercy he saved us...that being justified by his grace, we should be made heirs according to the hope of eternal life" (Titus 3:5-7). God's gift by His grace is rejected by any attempt to make even a partial payment.

That good deeds cannot pay for sins is not only biblical but logical. Even a traffic ticket cannot be paid on that basis. It will not avail to ask the judge to dismiss the charge for speeding because the guilty party has driven more often within the speed limit than he has exceeded it. Nor would the judge waive the payment of some crime in response to the defendant's promise never, ever to break the law again. The judge would simply say, "If you never break the law again you are only doing what the law demands. You receive no *extra* credit by which to pay for having broken the law in the past. That penalty is a separate issue and must be paid as prescribed."

The Bible further asserts that God's justice is infinite and that man being finite could never pay the infinite penalty it demands. We would be separated from God forever if we tried to work off the debt owed to His justice. God, being infinite, could pay that infinite penalty, but it wouldn't be just because He is not one of us. Therefore, God became a man through the virgin birth in order to take upon Himself, in our place, the judgment we deserve. And it is *only* on the basis of that penalty having been paid in full that God can offer forgiveness.

How amazing that religions which rely upon good works and rituals are considered to be "faiths." Faith can only engage the unseen and eternal and therefore does not mix with works and ritual. In search of a serious faith, it is folly to look at that which is visible. Even to look to a visible cross or crucifix is of no merit. What occurred on the cross for our salvation was invisible and must be accepted by faith.

The visible torture Christ endured, the scourging and mocking and nailing to the cross, is not the basis of our salvation. There is no virtue in making the "sign of the cross" or waving a cross or crucifix to ward off Satan or evil. It was the judgment Christ endured at the hands of God in payment of the penalty for our sins that makes it possible for God to offer salvation. That suffering, endured by Christ, was totally invisible to man and must ever be. It is by faith alone that we believe Christ paid the penalty and we receive the eternal salvation He offers.

The Bible speaks of "*the faith* which was once [for all time] delivered unto the saints" and declares that we must "earnestly contend" for this unchangeable truth because there are false teachers even inside the church who will seek through subterfuge to oppose it (Jude 3,4). Jude is not referring to believing that a prayer will be answered or an event will occur. *The faith* is the body of truth which must be believed for one to be a Christian.

The Bible allows for no compromise, no discussion, no dialogue with the world's religions (remember, Christianity is not a religion but distinct from all of them) in search for common ground. There is no common ground as far as God, Jesus Christ, and salvation are concerned. The very suggestion that dialogue may be appropriate denies that "the faith" has unique doctrinal content as a definitive body of truth for which we must earnestly contend, and opens the door to compromise in the interest of public relations.

Jesus didn't say, "Go into all the world and dialogue about faith." He said, "Go ye into all the world, and preach the gospel..." (Mark 16:15). Paul didn't dialogue with the rabbis and philosophers and pagan priests. He *"disputed* in the synagogue with the Jews, and with the devout persons, and in the market daily..." (Acts 17:17). Because he was angry and argumentative? No, because the eternal destiny of his hearers depended upon whether they believed or rejected the gospel.

A serious faith must take very seriously what Jesus said. Not what somebody says about what Jesus said, but His very words as recorded in the Bible. And we must face this truth for ourselves, not look to someone else to interpret it for us, no matter what credentials that person or church or institution might claim qualifies them to think for us. We must arrive at this serious faith ourselves, for serious faith is between each individual and God.

4

Concerning Prayer

But as for me, my prayer is unto thee,
O LORD...
—PSALM 69:13

The major partner to faith is prayer. Most people (religious or not, and even professed atheists), when desperate enough, have devoted at least some time and effort to prayer. Generally, prayer is thought to be a religious technique for talking some "god" or "higher power" into giving the petitioner what he or she wants. Few indeed are those who truly know God and sincerely pray, "Not my will but Thine be done." That attitude, however, necessarily belongs to those who by faith are confident that God truly loves them, is wiser than they are, and therefore His will would be infinitely better than their own.

In attempting to use prayer to get their own way, those who pray (including many who call themselves Christians) try very hard to drum up "faith," imagining that the key to answered prayer is to somehow *believe* the answer will come. If, however, believing brings to pass what one is praying for, then one doesn't need God. If that were the case, one could, by simply believing, bring into existence whatever one wanted without regard to any god.

And if that can be done, why bother with prayer at all? Why not simply affirm repeatedly what one desires? In fact, that is exactly what many people do, even those who are not at all religious. Positive affirmations play a large part in motivational and success seminars in the business world. If those who follow this practice, however, are willing to be honest with themselves, they must admit that this method is largely unsuccessful—for which we should all be thankful. How frightening it would be, and what chaos would reign, if everyone had the power to impose his or her will on the universe and upon the rest of mankind by affirming personal desires.

It is irrational to believe that affirmations will cause something to occur in the real world. What is the mechanism or universal law by which someone's belief or affirmation controls the course of events? The power of one's own mind? The desire for which one prays or makes affirmations to bend events to one's will almost inevitably involves factors which are interconnected to other people's lives. Why should one person's desires be imposed upon others? And what god or force would so readily accommodate individual passions?

> Prayer is petitioning God and must therefore be subject to His will.

Suppose several firmly held beliefs and affirmations of different individuals are in direct conflict, as many of them inevitably must be. What then? Which one will this universal mechanism or law allow? And, indeed, how can a mechanism or law decide anything? In fact, an impersonal principle cannot make choices or distinctions, so every affirmation would have to be granted. Here we see a major problem with this theory: If unlimited power were made available to everyone, the result would not be peace and blessing but increased conflict between human egos, resulting in even greater chaos than we already have on earth. Surely, if answers to prayer are to come, one would hope that a Supreme Intelligence is in charge of the process.

Jesus said, "Have faith in God" (Mark 11:22). The God revealed in the Bible does not exist to give us what we want. He is not a cosmic bellhop or genie in a bottle to grant wishes upon demand, though that is the only god many desire. Faith is not a force we aim at God to get Him to bend to our will and cater to our wants. According to Jesus, the object of faith must be the one true God and His truth. Prayer is petitioning God and must therefore be subject to His will.

Faith is not managing somehow to believe one's prayer will be answered. That would be mind power. Faith is believing that *God* will grant one's request. That fact changes everything. What we are praying for may not be God's will, God's way, or in God's time. There is a huge difference between demanding what we desire and trusting God to give us what He knows we need. Scripture declares: "Ye ask, and receive not, because ye ask amiss, that ye may consume it upon your lusts" (James 4:3).

The implication is that God refuses to grant requests for self-gratification. Prayer is not a technique for getting one's own way, but an appeal to the Creator, who is still in charge of His universe. But can't He be persuaded? God does reward earnestness. We are told to persist in prayer, no doubt to develop our character rather than to persuade Him. Would we really want to persuade God to bend His will to ours? It is right here that much misunderstanding about prayer causes so many to be disappointed or even disillusioned.

Jesus said, "Whatsoever ye shall ask the Father in my name, he will give it you" (John 16:23). Is this like "open sesame"? Obviously, to ask in Christ's name must mean more than just speaking out His name like a magic password for getting what we want. The ambassador who represents the United States in a foreign country has the right to use the

> True faith, as Jesus taught it, comes from knowing God and trusting Him.

name and authority of this country, but not for his own ends. The business manager representing a multimillionaire has power of attorney which gives him the right to use his employer's name, even to sign contracts and large checks. However, any use of the other's name is to be in the interest and for the benefit of that one, not for the benefit of his subordinate agent.

It would be fraud for the employee to enrich himself through the use of his employer's name. Yet Christians by the millions imagine that they can use the name of Jesus to their own ends. To ask in the name of Jesus is to ask as Jesus would ask in fulfillment of the Father's will and to His glory. Who would want it otherwise except an egomaniac so ignorant of his own selfishness and folly as to imagine that he could manage the universe better than God?

Of course, the God whom we petition cannot be a stranger (it would be folly to trust a stranger) or One from whom we are alienated. He must be One whom we know and with whom we have a right relationship. True faith, as Jesus taught it, comes from knowing God and trusting Him. Indeed, faith itself is a gift from God which He bestows on those who desire to know and do His will. To seek an answer to prayer that is contrary to God's will would be raw rebellion.

Still, the idea persists that faith is believing something strongly enough to make it happen. This delusion is usually found among those who imagine they hold to a scientific religion. Science works according to consistent laws. It is commonly taught, especially by those in the so-called faith movement, that there is a "law of faith" which works like gravity or thermodynamics, and if we obey that law, what we desire will be granted as automatically as the reaction between chemicals in a test tube.

This belief has at least four problems: (1) the Christian is "not under the law, but under grace" (Romans 6:14), yet grace has no part to play in this supposed law of faith; (2) the Bible never even hints that the realm of the spirit is governed by laws similar to those governing the physical realm; (3) the physical laws God has established are intended to *control* man (even Adam and Eve were subject to them) and to *limit* what we can do with God's universe, but this presumed law of faith does just the opposite. It allows each person to become a "god" waving a magic wand over the physical universe—and thus does not fit the pattern of laws which God has established; and (4) the very heart of the prayer pattern Jesus taught His disciples is, "Thy kingdom come. Thy will be done, in earth as it is in heaven" (Matthew 6:10), but the law of faith would accomplish just the opposite, gaining for man the accomplishment of his will. Indeed, the teachers in this movement insist that it destroys faith to pray "if it be thy [God's] will."

Very similar to the faith movement within charismatic and Pentecostal circles is the New Thought Alliance of churches. Although they are far outside biblical Christianity, most claim to be Christian and many of their teachings are similar to those of the faith movement. Popular groups involved include Christian Science, Religious Science, Science of Mind, and Unity as well as many independent churches not directly affiliated with any of these. And how do they think their affirmations turn into reality? They propose an all-powerful universal Mind which exists to serve mankind. Oddly, this great Mind apparently has no mind of its own but is ever ready to turn wishes into horses so everyone can ride who knows how to tap into this ever available power. Only the human ego mimicking Satan could come up with such a self-centered concept.

Hinduism holds to a similar belief. It denies objective reality and claims that we have created with our minds an imaginary universe called *maya*. By changing our thinking, we can change our universe. One sees bumper stickers which apparently reflect the same wishful belief: "Think Snow," or "Think Peace." And at least some of those who display these slogans actually believe the united thinking of enough people can literally create snow or peace or anything else that is desired.

Positive Mental Attitude (PMA) seminars and much success training in the business world involve a similar fantasy— the idea that we can create success by holding thoughts of success in our minds. The same is true of the teaching of Positive Thinking and Possibility Thinking which have gained a wide following among professing Christians and even among evangelicals. According to their chief proponents, Positive Thinking and Possibility Thinking are actually synonymous with faith. On the contrary, atheists can and do teach Positive/Possibility Thinking seminars. No atheist, however, can have biblical faith, which is *in God*. Nor has He, thankfully, put His universe and our lives at the mercy of our badly flawed "positive" thinking.

Serious faith is absolute, unquestioning trust in God and in His love, wisdom, and will. Trusting in another's wisdom and integrity is something which all of us, whether atheist, agnostic, or religionist, must do many times each day. We go to a doctor, who makes a diagnosis we can't understand even when he explains it. He writes out a prescription in a hand we can't decipher and couldn't comprehend even if we could read it. We take that to a pharmacist, who puts together compounds with mysterious names totally foreign to our understanding. Yet we ingest the medicine because we trust our doctor for the promised results.

We don't force our way into the cockpit of the commercial aircraft we're flying to look over the pilots' shoulders to make certain they are doing their job. We don't know how to fly that aircraft and we have no choice but to trust the flying to them. Nor do we look over the mechanic's shoulder as he tunes our engine, or stay up all night to make certain that the baker puts the right ingredients into the bread we purchase. Clearly, in the progress of daily affairs, we must constantly rely upon experts who know what we don't know and can do what we can't do.

Such trust is essential because we can't know everything we need to know even to be moderately successful in life on this earth, much less to surmount every difficulty and solve every problem we will face in our threescore years and ten. Unfortunately, all of us at times have been hurt one way or another by reliance upon a supposed expert who made a costly mistake either because he or she was incompetent or was only human, and to err is human. Fortunately, no matter how serious such mishaps may be, we can usually recover—though often with great cost and difficulty and only after much time. When it comes to eternal matters, however, such recovery is not possible once we have passed through death's door.

There are many self-professed "experts" in spiritual matters. They claim to know about heaven and hell but have never been there. They generally offer weak reasons for trusting them: they have degrees from a seminary, they've been ordained by some religious body, they've been voted in to a position of authority by a committee, they've written some books, their denomination is the oldest or largest, their church the only correct one and outside of it there is no salvation, they are apostles or prophets and get continuing revelations from God, and so on. None of these reasons can be the basis of a serious faith. Where is the evidence that they should be believed and we should therefore follow them into eternity? We dare not take that trip without absolute certainty.

The gravest error associated with prayer is to imagine that it is essential for salvation. On the contrary, as we have seen from many scriptures, God offers salvation as a free gift. When a gift is offered, one does not beg for it, plead for it, or agonize for it. One simply receives it. To beg or plead or pray for the gift is to betray one's lack of faith in the giver and his offer.

In order to get serious about faith, one must realize that faith is not a magic wand we wave to get what we want. Far from having some power within itself, faith must have an object. There are two essential ingredients in faith: *what* one believes and *in whom* one believes.

Faith can either fulfill or disappoint. Remember, faith is in the invisible and eternal and thus determines one's eternal destiny. Obviously, to believe what is false about eternity and the God of eternity is to set oneself up for eternal loss and remorse. No tragedy could be greater.

5

Shortcut
to Truth

I have even from the beginning declared
it to thee; before it came to pass
I showed it thee.
—ISAIAH 48:5

If what one believes cannot *create* reality, then belief must be *derived* from reality. Yet the belief of so many, particularly in the area of religion, has no factual foundation. The beliefs of many religious people are little more than sanctified superstitions. Many either do not want to face any evidence to the contrary ("I never discuss religion!") or imagine that faith is proved to be all the stronger if it stands firm in the face of evidence that contradicts it. Obviously, however, a "faith" that is not based upon truth cannot be defended and should not be relied upon. It can only lead one day to taking a final leap into the dark.

Where is truth and certainty to be found? Shall we devote our lives to studying all of the world's religions in an attempt to find the right one? No one could live long enough to complete that task. Then how can one make a valid decision

> We can prove beyond the shadow of a doubt that every word in the Bible is true.

without knowing all of the choices available?

There is a simple solution, a shortcut to truth: start with the Bible first and investigate it thoroughly. Why start there? Not just because the Bible claims to be the only inspired Word of the one true God who created us. It also claims that all of the world's religions and their scriptures are false and actually in the service of Satan. The Bible calls Satan "the god of this world" (2 Corinthians 4:4) and thus the author of its religions. So if the Bible is true, we have saved ourselves a lifetime of vain searching through false systems.

In fact, we can prove beyond the shadow of a doubt that every word in the Bible is true. Entire books by many authors offer this proof in detail. We have also presented it extensively in other writings. Here we can only provide enough information for each reader to be able to study further in order to confirm the absolute truth of the Bible to his or her own satisfaction.

The Bible has several unique features not found in the scriptures of the world's religions which make it possible to substantiate its claims. Christianity is not a philosophy, mystical experience, or esoteric practice. Nor are the major doctrines of Christianity a matter of mere dogma and belief. They are intricately tied into established history. In contrast to the world's religions, all of which are based to a large extent upon legends, Christianity alone is based upon undeniable and historical facts. Its doctrines can thus be evaluated on the basis of evidence.

Furthermore, many of the Bible's major events and teachings were prophesied centuries and even thousands of years beforehand in understandable language. Their actual fulfillment is part of recorded world history. Thus, the Bible stands upon a four-fold foundation, every part of which can be examined and verified: 1) prophecy foretelling events and doctrines in advance, 2) fulfillment of those prophecies in detail, 3) secular history testifying to the fulfillment of prophecies and events, and 4) factual data corroborated by archaeology and science. None of this is the case with the teachings or scriptures of any of the world's religions.

Such differences set the Bible apart as absolutely unique. In fact, Christianity, which is based upon the Bible, cannot even be counted among the religions of the world. Christianity does not seek accommodation, much less partnership, with world religions; it seeks their overthrow as hopelessly false and destructive to mankind. That may come as a shock to some readers, but it is the clear teaching of the Bible. Christ Himself, as we have already quoted, denounced as "thieves and robbers" all who sought to get to heaven except through Him.

Each religion offers a system of belief and practice taught by its founder whereby one supposedly gains acceptance with God. No religion claims that its founder died for the sins of the world and was resurrected. Nor is it essential that the founder of any of the world's religions be alive. Christianity, on the other hand, depends entirely upon Christ Himself having died for our sins and being resurrected and presently alive to live by His Spirit within His followers. Jesus said, "Because I live, ye shall live also" (John 14:19).

Unique to the Bible is its authorship. It was written by some 40 different men over a period of about 1,600 years. Living in different cultures and at different times in history, most of them never knew one another. Yet the Bible comprises one coherent message from Genesis to Revelation—without any contradictions. The continuity and remarkable content of the message can only be explained by inspiration from a supernatural Source. New revelation through subsequent prophets is always consistent with what went before, supplementing, enlarging, and building upon it.

These 40 authors had only this in common, that each claimed to be inspired by God. If this claim is not true, the Bible is the greatest fraud imaginable and has done incalculable harm to millions. Yet it bears the unmistakable stamp of truth in many verifiable ways, and its unequaled moral effect for good could hardly be the fruit of fraud.

The oldest part of the biblical text dates back about 3,500 years and the newest about 1,900 years, yet it remains as valid and relevant as when it was written. Not a word or concept is outdated by the progress of civilization or science. One can find no other literature of the same time period of which that can be said.

There is not one word in the Bible that reflects the ignorance or superstition of the culture or the time in which it was written. Moses, for example, who wrote the first five books of the Bible, lived around 1600 B.C. He was raised in pharaoh's palace and given the best education available in the Egypt of that day. That means he was schooled in many grossly unscientific notions which were fully believed by pharaoh's counselors at that time. Yet not one of these errors appears in the writings of Moses. Instead, there is a wisdom and understanding foreign to, and far beyond, the culture of that time—something which could not possibly be the case had he not, as he claimed, been inspired of God in what he wrote.

To a large extent, the hygienic laws God gave Israel through Moses preserved Jewish communities during the Middle Ages from the various plagues which swept through the civilized world. Jews were even persecuted because they seemed immune and therefore were accused of putting this curse on the Gentile populace. It took medicine more than 3,000 years to catch up to Moses even in something so simple as the need to wash one's hands. It was only a few decades ago that the preventive health benefits of circumcision which God gave to Abraham nearly 4,000 years ago were recognized by the medical profession. Only recently was it also discovered that on the eighth day after birth, the day prescribed for circumcision, the clotting factor in the newborn's blood, having dropped right after birth, is at the highest level that it will ever be.

The Bible is not a book of science. It deals with something far more important. It does, however, make many factual statements about the universe which reflect a wisdom far beyond the time and culture in which it was written. Some of these insights have only recently been confirmed by modern science and none of them has been proved wrong. That in itself is a remarkable witness to inspiration not found in other scriptures.

For comparison, read anything written at the same time the books of the Old Testament (or of the New) were written. The difference is as great as night and day. The Qur'an, for example, which was written more than 2,000 years after the earliest books in the Bible, contains numerous unscientific statements and superstitions, and treats primitive Arab custom in dress and diet of Muhammad's time as inspired by Allah and obligatory upon Muslims even today.

The contrast between other scriptures, which reflect the superstitious, unscientific views of their time, and the supernatural validity of the Bible cannot be denied. In a day when it was believed that the earth sat on the back of a tortoise floating in a cosmic sea, the Bible said God "hangeth the earth upon nothing" (Job 26:7). What it says about clouds and rain is remarkable: "He [God] bindeth up the waters in his thick clouds...[and maketh] a way for the lightning...to cause it to rain on the earth" (Job 26:8; 38:25,26). Molecules of water are, in fact, *bound* together in a way which is unique among all substances. Indeed, it is this peculiar molecular bonding which allows clouds and raindrops to form. Moreover, as the Bible says, the electric charge connected with lightning plays a key role in causing rain. These facts were only discovered in this century, yet the Bible stated them 3,500 years ago. Many similar examples could be given.

The Bible deals accurately with the history, location, and geography of many nations, countries, and cities. For example, 29 of the ancient kings mentioned in the Bible are also named on monuments of their time, some dating back 4,000 years. Of the 195 consonants in their names, there are only 2 or 3 which could be questioned as to whether they are written in the Bible exactly as on the monuments. By comparison, the greatest scholar of his day, the librarian at Alexandria, Egypt, in 200 B.C., refers to 38 Egyptian kings, of which only 3 or 4 are recognizable. Of the Assyrian kings he lists, only one is identifiable and it isn't spelled correctly. In the list Ptolemy made of 18 Babylonian kings, not one is spelled properly and none could be identified without help from other sources. Yet in the Bible, each of the 29 kings from 10 countries has his complicated name spelled correctly, and each is given his right place and time in history. Such accuracy in every detail reinforces the truth of the doctrines being taught at the same time.

No other scriptures have been critically investigated like the Bible. It has been under the skeptics' microscopes for centuries and analyzed from every conceivable angle by critics determined to discredit it. None of the scriptures of any of the world's religions has been subjected to comparable scrutiny, nor could they withstand it if they were. Even a cursory reading of scriptures other than the Bible reveals multiple errors of fact, history, and science.

Yes, critics have often claimed to have found errors in the Bible based upon what was known at the time. When further facts have been discovered, however, the Bible has proved to be 100 percent accurate and the critics wrong. For example, earlier in this century, it was claimed that the Hittite peoples, given prominent mention in the Bible (as strong and numerous from the time of Abraham to David), had never existed. Later, the archaeological evidence began to pour in. Today, there is an entire museum in Ankara, Turkey, devoted to the Hittites and filled with proof that what the Bible said about them was accurate.

Great museums around the world display masses of evidence fully supporting what the Bible has to say. In comparison, consider the Book of Mormon. For decades, at the cost of millions of dollars, the Mormon Church has maintained an aggressive archaeological program literally scouring North, Central, and South America in search of evidence to support the Book of Mormon. To date they have not found so much as a pin or coin or stone or inscription. There is no evidence whatsoever that any of the cities described in the Book of Mormon ever existed. Even the geography can't be verified. The same is true of the *Bhagavad-Gita* and other Hindu writings, or the legends of various indigenous peoples around the world. Israeli students, however, study the history of their country and ancestors from the Bible and archaeologists use the Bible as a guide for locating the buried ruins of ancient cities.

Furthermore, only the Bible has written history centuries and even thousands of years before it happened. It is this fact, above all, which puts the Bible in a class of its own. Its many plainly stated prophecies (not in guarded, ambiguous language like the French quatrains of a Nostradamus) were recorded centuries and even thousands of years before their accurate fulfillment. These prophecies are so numerous, stated in perfect agreement by so many different prophets who had no contact with one another, and many of them so unlikely ever to happen, given the normal course of events, that the probability of fulfillment by chance is infinitely remote. This fact simply cannot be explained away by the skeptics on any rational basis. One is forced from this evidence alone to admit the supernatural origin of the Bible.

> The God of the Bible reminds us that He alone declares what will happen in advance and that its fulfillment proves that He is the only true God.

There are no prophecies of verifiable date of origin and documented fulfillment centuries later—*not one*—in the Qur'an, in the Hindu Vedas, in the sayings of Buddha, in the sayings of Confucius, or in any other scriptures of the world's religions. The Bible, however, is about twenty-eight percent prophecy, and its thousands of prophecies cover a wide range of subjects and events.

Some biblical prophecy (the rapture of the church, the revealing of Antichrist and establishment of his world government, the Great Tribulation, Armageddon, the Second

Coming of Christ to rescue Israel) awaits future fulfillment. Most Bible prophecies, however, have *already* been fulfilled, and these comprise irrefutable proof that the Bible is the inspired Word of God. Repeatedly, the God of the Bible reminds us that He alone declares what will happen in advance and that its fulfillment proves that He is the only true God. For example:

> Behold, the former things [I foretold through my prophets] are come to pass, and new things do I declare: before they spring forth I tell you of them.
>
> I am God, and there is none like me, declaring the end from the beginning, and from ancient times the things that are not yet done, saying, My counsel shall stand, and I will do all my pleasure.
>
> I have even from the beginning declared it to thee; before it came to pass I showed it thee: lest thou shouldest say, Mine idol hath done them.... (Isaiah 42:9; 46:9,10; 48:5)

There are two major topics of prophecy in the Bible: Israel and the Messiah who comes to Israel and through Israel to the world. There are hundreds of prophecies concerning Israel, God's chosen people, which have been fulfilled, and many more are in the process of fulfillment, as we are witnessing in our day. The fulfillment of prophecies concerning Israel comprise vital parts of history acknowledged by the entire world. Below is a brief outline.

According to the Bible, God gave the land of Israel exclusively to His chosen people, the Jews. It was specifically promised to the descendants of "Abraham, Isaac, and Jacob." Israel was the new name given by God to Jacob, and it is from this name that the Promised Land derives its proper title to this day. The importance of these people can be seen in the fact that God tells Moses, "I am...the God of Abraham, the God of Isaac, and the God of Jacob...this is my name for ever, and this is my memorial unto all generations" (Exodus 3:6,15). The Bible identifies God in this way twelve times, the number of the tribes of Israel.

The descendants of Abraham, Isaac, and Jacob, known as "the children of Israel," were led to the Promised Land by Moses nearly 3,500 years ago. At that time, God warned His people through Moses that they would disobey Him and because of that He would scatter them to every part of this world, where they would be hated, persecuted, and slaughtered as no other people. What we now identify as anti-Semitism was foretold in detail by numerous prophets. At the same time, God promised to preserve the Jews as an identifiable ethnic people and to bring them, in the last days, back into their own land of Israel. No non-Jews, whether Arabs or any other nationality, have any claim upon that land, which God has promised to defend.

Through the prophet Zechariah, God declared that in the last days preceding Christ's Second Coming, when the Jews had been restored to the Promised Land, Jerusalem would be like a millstone around the necks of the nations. Today it is the world's major problem; a nuclear war could break out at any time over that Holy City. In remarkable fulfillment of prophecy, the United Nations Security Council has devoted nearly one-third of its deliberations and resolutions to Israel, a country with less than one-thousandth of the earth's population. That would not be the case were it not for the fulfillment of another amazing prophecy: that tiny Israel would be so powerful militarily that she would defeat the surrounding nations that would attack her.

Israel's history is the unfolding of prophecy fulfilled exactly as foretold in the Bible—and more is to come. Yet to be fulfilled in the near future are prophecies declaring that Israel will be forced into making a false peace that will set her up for an attack by all the nations of the world under the leadership of Antichrist. Current events seem to be heading in that direction and leading to Armageddon. That horrible war will bring the intervention of Jesus Christ from heaven to rescue Israel and to destroy Antichrist and his world government. All indications today are that we are indeed heading toward a world government.

The Bible declares that Antichrist will control all banking and commerce in the entire world with a number, a remarkable prophecy anticipating modern computer technology. Furthermore, Christ declared that if He did not stop Armageddon, no one would be left alive on earth—another astonishing prophecy which anticipated today's incredibly destructive weapons, unknown to past generations.

There are thousands of verses in the Bible dealing with Israel. Prophecies pertaining to Israel are a major part of the Christian Scriptures. Yet nothing about the great events foretold in the Bible concerning Israel is found in the writings of any of the world's religions. Nor do they contain any prophecies concerning Israel's Messiah—nor even for any of their founders. There are no verifiable and clear prophecies foretelling the coming of Buddha, Confucius, Muhammad, Zoroaster, the Bab, Baha'ullah, and others in any scriptures.

But for the Jewish Messiah, there are literally hundreds of specific prophecies, all of which were undeniably fulfilled in the life, death, and resurrection of Jesus of Nazareth. The Bible prophesied where Christ would be born and that He would be betrayed for 30 pieces of silver and rejected by His own people. The exact date of the *very day* the Messiah would ride into Jerusalem, that He would be hailed as the Messiah though riding humbly on a donkey, then crucified four days later (foretold centuries before crucifixion was practiced on earth), and that He would rise from the dead the third day— these and many other details were also prophesied.

The fulfillment of numerous prophecies in the life, death, and resurrection of Jesus of Nazareth cannot be explained by coincidence and proves beyond dispute that He is the only Savior of mankind, exactly as He claimed to be. If Jesus did not fulfill, without exception, what the Hebrew prophets declared in the Scriptures concerning the coming of the promised Messiah, then no matter how appealing we may find His teaching and personality, He must be rejected.

Furthermore, that millions of non-Jews all over the world would become believers in the God of Israel, and that this would happen through their faith in the very Messiah whom the Jews would reject, was prophesied repeatedly by Hebrew prophets throughout the Old Testament. The rabbis and even Christ's disciples did not recognize these prophecies, not because the language was unclear, but because they were blinded by unbelief. That the conversion of hundreds of millions of Gentiles has happened in spite of the unbelief of the Jewish nation in their Messiah is one of the most remarkable events in history. Today, there are about 2 billion people who, though they are not all true Christians according to the standards Jesus set, claim to believe in Him and through Him to believe in the God of Abraham, Isaac, and Jacob.

Paul was not the inventor of Christianity, as some have claimed, nor even was Jesus. Christianity exists in fulfillment of hundreds of prophecies. Not only that there would be multitudes of Gentile believers, but the specifics of the doctrines of salvation were laid out clearly in the Old Testament. Christ Himself pointed to these prophecies, and Paul made them the basis of the gospel he preached. This is absolutely unique. There is no comparable verification for any of the doctrines of any of the world's religions.

Paul declared that "the gospel of God" he preached was backed up by the Old Testament. He begins his epistle to the Romans with these words: "Paul, a servant of Jesus Christ, called to be an apostle, separated unto the gospel of God (which he promised afore by his prophets in the holy scriptures,)..." (Romans 1:1,2). In every city Paul entered on his missionary journeys he went first of all into the synagogue and proved to the Jewish congregants that what their own prophets had foretold concerning the coming Messiah, Jesus Christ had fulfilled, including His death on the cross and His resurrection: "And Paul, as his manner was, went in unto them [in the synagogue], and three sabbath days reasoned with them out of the [Hebrew] scriptures, opening and alleging, that Christ must needs have suffered, and risen again from the dead; and that this Jesus, whom I preach unto you, is Christ" (Acts 17:2,3).

Christ did exactly the same. Scolding the two disheartened disciples walking to Emmaus from Jerusalem three days after His crucifixion, who knew the tomb was empty but didn't believe Christ had risen from the dead, He said: "O fools, and slow of heart to believe all that the prophets have spoken: ought not Christ to have suffered these things [i.e. rejection by Israel and crucifixion], and to enter into his glory? And beginning at Moses and all the prophets he expounded unto them in all the scriptures the things concerning himself" (Luke 24:25-27). He told His disciples repeatedly that "all things must be fulfilled, which were written in the law of Moses, and in the prophets, and in the psalms, concerning me" (Luke 24:44).

In the following pages we will offer, not our ideas, not the ideas of some church or religious leader, but what the Bible itself says about salvation and living the Christian life. Because of the irrefutable proof that it is God's Word, the Bible is our authority.

We commend the Bible to each reader. Do not take our word, but search God's Word for yourself. Why is this personal study necessary? Because to whatever extent one relies upon some third party (pastor, priest, preacher, author, church, etc.) to interpret the Bible, to that extent one has lost contact with God and His Word. God wants to speak to each individual through His Word and through Jesus Christ, not through some other intermediary.

The Bible itself says, "Faith cometh by hearing...the word of God" (Romans 10:17). In our urgent call for a serious faith we must turn to the Scriptures alone. It is then up to each one to check it all out from the Bible, the only infallible authority, and to believe the Word of God. Such is the basis of a serious faith, a faith that saves for eternity.

Part II

God's Good News

6

What Is
the Gospel?

Go ye into all the world, and preach
the gospel...for it is the power of God unto
salvation to every one that believeth [it].
—MARK 16:15; ROMANS 1:16

What is the gospel—and from what does it save us?

In order to answer that question, we must go back to the Garden. It was there, in the most perfect environment that God's heart of love and His creative power could design, that sin had its awful beginning.

Surrounded by beauty, satisfied by abundance, and enjoying the fellowship of their Creator Friend, our first parents, nevertheless, fell to the seductive lies of the serpent. "Ye shall be as gods" was Satan's promise. Though not deceived himself (1 Timothy 2:14), Adam, in loyalty to Eve, joined in his wife's disobedience and ate of the forbidden fruit. Thus, "by [this] one man sin entered into the world, and death by sin; and so death passed upon all men, for that all have sinned" (Romans 5:12).

Death not only ends this short earthly life, it separates the sinner from God forever. In His infinite foreknowledge, wisdom, and love, however, God had already planned how He would restore life and reunite mankind with Himself. Without ceasing to be God, He would become a man through a virgin birth. Only God could be the Savior (Isaiah 43:11; 45:21); thus the Messiah had to be God (Isaiah 9:6; 45:15; Titus 1:3,4). He would die for our sins to pay the penalty demanded by His own perfect justice: " 'Tis mystery all, the *Immortal* dies!" hymn writer Charles Wesley declared. Then He would rise from the dead to live in those who would believe in and receive Him as their Lord and Savior. Forgiveness of sins and eternal life would be theirs as a free gift of His grace—the only way man could receive it.

> "What must I do to be saved?...Believe on the Lord Jesus Christ, and thou shalt be saved."
> —Acts 16:30,31

Centuries before His incarnation, God inspired the Old Testament prophets to declare His eternal and unchangeable plan of salvation. Definitive criteria were provided by which the coming Savior would be identified. Jesus and His apostles did not invent a "new religion." Christianity fulfills scores of specific prophecies and is therefore provable from Scripture!

So it was not a new gospel which Paul the apostle preached, but "the gospel of God (which he had promised afore by his prophets in the holy scriptures) concerning his Son Jesus Christ..." (Romans 1:1-3). Thus the Bereans could check Paul's message against the Old Testament (Acts 17:11); and he could use the Hebrew prophets, which were read in the synagogue each Sabbath, to prove that Jesus was the promised Messiah (verses 2,3). Not Buddha, not Muhammad, not anyone else—only Jesus Christ has the required credentials. The fulfillment of scores of specific prophecies in the life, death, and resurrection of Jesus of Nazareth provide absolute proof that He is the true and only Savior.

In Hebrews 2:3 the vital question is asked, "How shall we escape, if we neglect so great salvation?" The answer is unequivocal: there is no escape. The Bible makes that solemn fact abundantly clear. To reject, add to, take from, or otherwise pervert or embrace a substitute for "the gospel of God" is to perpetuate the rebellion begun by Adam and Eve and to leave one eternally separated from God and His proffered salvation.

No wonder Paul wrote, "Knowing therefore the terror of the Lord, we persuade men..." (2 Corinthians 5:11). So must we, too, persuade men to believe the only gospel that saves!

The "gospel of your salvation" (Ephesians 1:13) "wherein ye stand; by which also ye are saved" (1 Corinthians 15:1,2) is simple and precise, leaving no room for misunderstanding or negotiation: "that Christ died for our sins according to the scriptures; and that he was buried, and that he rose again the third day according to the scriptures" (verses 3,4).

> "The gospel of Christ...is the power of God unto salvation to every one that believeth."
> —Romans 1:16

This "everlasting gospel" (Revelation 14:6) was promised "before the world began" (2 Timothy 1:9; Titus 1:2) and cannot change with time or culture. There is no other hope for mankind, no other way to be forgiven and brought back to God except through this "strait gate and narrow way" (Matthew 7:13,14). Any broader road leads to destruction according to Jesus Himself.

The one true "gospel of God's grace," which God offers as our *only* salvation, has three basic elements: 1) who Christ is—fully God and perfect, sinless man in one Person (were He less, He could not be our Savior), 2) who we are—hopeless sinners already condemned to eternal death (or we wouldn't need to be saved), and 3) what Christ's death accomplished—the payment of the full penalty for our sins (any attempt by us to pay *in any way* rejects the gift of salvation God offers).

Christ has commanded us to "preach the gospel [good news!] to every creature [person]" (Mark 16:15). What response is required? Both the desperate question and uncomplicated answer are given to us: "What must I do to be saved? ...Believe on the Lord Jesus Christ, and thou shalt be saved" (Acts 16:30,31). Neither religion, ritual, nor good works will avail—God calls us to simply believe. "For by grace are ye saved through faith" (Ephesians 2:8)—"whosoever believes in him will not perish, but has eternal life" (John 3:16).

It is the gospel alone that saves those who believe it. Nothing else will save. Therefore we must preach the gospel. Paul said, "Woe is unto me, if I preach not the gospel" (1 Corinthians 9:16). Sentimental appeals to "come to Jesus" or "make a decision for Christ" avail nothing if the gospel is not clearly explained and believed.

Many are attracted to Christ because of His admirable character, noble martyrdom, or because He changes lives. If that is all they see in Christ, such converts have not believed the gospel and thus are not saved. This is the solemn teaching of Scripture (John 3:36).

Paul said that "the gospel of Christ...is the power of God unto salvation to every one that believeth" (Romans 1:16). He also called it "the gospel...by which also ye are saved" (1 Corinthians 15:1,2); and "the gospel of your salvation" (Ephesians 1:13). Clearly, from these and other scriptures, salvation comes only through believing the gospel. Christ told His disciples to go into "all the world, and preach the gospel" (Mark 16:15), a gospel which the Bible precisely defines.

Salvation comes on God's terms and by His grace, and we negotiate the gospel neither with God nor with one another. "The Father sent the Son to be the Saviour of the world" (1 John 4:14). Salvation is a work of God and His Son. We either believe it or reject it. We don't "dialogue" about it.

It is also called the "gospel of Christ" (Mark 1:1; Romans 1:16; 15:19; 1 Corinthians 9:12). He is the Savior, and salvation is His work, not ours, as the angels said: "For unto you is born this day in the city of David a Saviour, which is Christ the Lord" (Luke 2:11).

Paul specifies the gospel that saves: "that Christ died for our sins according to the scriptures; and that he was buried, and that he rose again the third day according to the scriptures" (1 Corinthians 15:3,4). "I am the door," said Christ: "By *me* if any man enter in, he shall be saved" (John 10:9).

The gospel contains nothing about baptism, church membership or attendance, tithing, sacraments or rituals, diet or clothing. If we add *anything* to the gospel, we have perverted it and thus come under Paul's anathema in Galatians 1:8,9.

The gospel is all about what Christ has done. It says nothing about what Christ must yet do, because the work of our redemption is finished. "Christ *died* for our sins" (1 Corinthians 15:3). His death on the cross is in the past, never to be repeated, for Christ triumphantly declared, "It is *finished*" (John 19:30)!

Nor does the gospel say anything about what *we* must do, because we can do nothing. "Not by works of righteousness which we have done, but according to his mercy he saved us" (Titus 3:5); "for by grace are ye saved, through faith...the gift of God [is] not of works, lest any man should boast" (Ephesians 2:8,9).

Instead of works, the gospel requires faith. It is the power of God unto salvation to those who *believe*. "Now to him that *worketh not*, but *believeth* on him that justifieth the ungodly, his *faith* is counted for righteousness" (Romans 4:5)..."that whosoever believeth in him should not perish, but have everlasting life" (John 3:16).

The gospel is a two-edged sword. It declares, "He that believeth on the Son hath everlasting life." The same verse also says, "he that believeth not the Son shall not see life; but the wrath of God abideth on him" (John 3:36).

Right here we come to the most difficult part of the gospel to accept: that those who do not believe it are eternally lost—no matter what good works they do.

The reasons for that fact are grounded in both God's love and His justice. God's justice requires that the infinite penalty for sin must be paid. For us to pay would separate us from God forever, so He became a man through the virgin birth to pay the penalty for us. No one can complain against God. He has proved His love by doing all He could for our salvation. He has Himself paid the penalty, and on that basis can be both "just, and the justifier of him which believeth in Jesus" (Romans 3:26).

Christ pleaded in the Garden, "If it be possible [that is, if there is any other way mankind can be saved], let this cup pass from me" (Matthew 26:39). We know that there is no other way, or God would not have required His beloved Son to bear the full brunt of His wrath against sin. That men nailed Christ to the cross is not the basis of our salvation. That heinous act would only add to our condemnation. But on the cross, when man was doing his worst to his Creator, Christ paid the penalty for our sins in full.

Only if we accept that payment on our behalf can we be saved. "[T]here is none other name under heaven given among men, whereby we *must* be saved" (Acts 4:12); "what *must* I do to be saved?...Believe on the Lord Jesus Christ, and thou shalt be saved" (Acts 16:30,31).

To "believe on the Lord Jesus Christ" includes *who He is* and *what He has done.*

Jesus said, "Ye are from beneath; I am from above...if ye believe not that *I am*...[I AM is God's name, Jahweh], ye shall die in your sins" (John 8:23,24). Jesus Himself says we must believe that He is God, for He is; and no one less than God could save us. We must believe that the sinless One "died for our sins," and was buried, and that He rose bodily from the grave. Only by believing this gospel are we saved. So says God's Word.

But wouldn't the exceptional good works of a Mother Teresa get her to heaven? No. Because we are all sinners, including Mother Teresa. Once we have broken one of God's commandments we are "guilty of all" (James 2:10). Furthermore, "by the deeds of the law there shall no flesh be justified in his sight" (Romans 3:20). Keeping the law perfectly from now on could never make up for having already broken it. Good works, no matter *how* good, can never pay for sin.

For God to grant salvation by any other means than faith in Christ alone would be an insult to the One whom the Father insisted had to endure His wrath as the sacrifice for sin. Moreover, if He did so, God would be breaking His own code of justice and going back on His Word. Not even God Himself could save earth's most notable "saint." Christ's blood avails only for repentant sinners.

Oswald Chambers warned lest, in our zeal to get people to accept the gospel, we manufacture a gospel acceptable to people and produce "converts" who are not saved. Today's most popular perversion is the "positive" gospel, which is designed to offend no one with truth. One of our most popular televangelists, for example, has said that it is demeaning to call anyone a sinner and that Christ died to restore human dignity and self-esteem. He claims to win many to Christ with that seductive message—but such a gospel does not save sinners.

Evangelistic appeals are often made to "come to Christ" for the wrong reasons: in order to be healthy, happy, or successful; to restore a marriage; or to handle stress. Others preach a gospel that is so diluted or perverted that it deceives many into thinking they are saved. No fraud could be worse, for the consequences are eternal!

Religion, not atheism, is Satan's main weapon. "The god of this world hath blinded the minds of them which believe not, lest the light of the glorious gospel of Christ...should shine unto them" (2 Corinthians 4:4). To pervert "the gospel of the grace of God" (Acts 20:24), the great deceiver offers many false gospels, but they all have two subtle rejections of grace in common: ritual and/or self-effort.

Ritual makes redemption an ongoing process performed by a special priesthood, and self-effort gives man a part to play in earning his salvation. The one denies the finality of the cross. The other denies its sufficiency. Either one robs

God of the uniqueness of the gift He wishes to bestow upon fallen man: "The wages of sin is death; but the gift of God is eternal life through Jesus Christ our Lord" (Romans 6:23).

One can only *receive* a gift. Any attempt to earn, merit, or pay for a gift, even in part, is to reject it. Furthermore, God wants to personally give us this gift of eternal life through Jesus Christ. To look to a church, organization, or some religious leader to dispense God's gift is to reject it from His hand. Jesus said, "Come into *me...I* give my sheep eternal life...I am the door; by *me* if any man enter in he shall be saved..." (Matthew 11:28; John 10:27,28,9).

Faith must be in God and in Christ alone. To place it anywhere else is to admit a lack of faith in Him. Let us together get serious about faith by searching out and believing what God has said. Therein lies our only authority and assurance.

7

Mercy vs. Works

*An altar of earth thou shalt make unto me...And
if thou wilt make me an altar of stone, thou shalt
not build it of hewn stone: for if thou lift up thy
tool upon it, thou has polluted it. Neither shalt
thou go up by steps unto mine altar, that thy
nakedness be not discovered thereon.*
—EXODUS 20:24-26

*Let us build us a city and a tower [of Babel],
whose top may reach unto heaven.*
—GENESIS 11:4

No two tenets of faith could be more opposed to one
another than those presented above.

On the one hand, we have God's rejection of any human
effort to buy salvation or His favor. If man is to come to God,
it must be solely by God's grace and provision, not by any
human work.

On the other hand, we see man's flagrant repudiation of
God's prohibition against self-effort and his arrogant attempt
to build a tower that would enable him to climb by steps of
his own making into heaven itself.

> "For by grace are ye saved...not of works, lest any man should boast."
> —Ephesians 2:8,9
>
> "Not by works of righteousness which we have done, but according to his mercy he saved us."
> —Titus 3:5

God's instructions were explicit. If the ground was too rocky to gather up a mound of earth for an altar, stones could be heaped together—but they could not be cut, fashioned, or polished with a tool. Nor could the altar be elevated. Not one step must be climbed to reach it. There must be no illusion that man could contribute anything by his own efforts to his salvation. God Himself is the only One who can save man, and salvation must be a gift of His grace. Such is the gospel consistently preached from Genesis to Revelation. Consider the following:

> *I, even I, am the LORD; and beside me there is no saviour* (Isaiah 43:11).
> *For unto us a child [the Messiah] is born...[He is] The mighty God, The everlasting Father* (Isaiah 9:6).
> *Thou shalt call his name JESUS; for he shall save his people from their sins* (Matthew 1:21).
> *They that are in the flesh cannot please God* (Romans 8:8).
> *For by grace are ye saved...not of works, lest any man should boast* (Ephesians 2:8,9).
> *Not by works of righteousness which we have done, but according to his mercy he saved us* (Titus 3:5).
> *Being justified freely by his grace through the redemption that is in Christ Jesus* (Romans 3:24).
> *And if by grace, then is it no more of works; otherwise grace is no more grace. But if it be of works, then is it no more grace: otherwise work is no more work* (Romans 11:6).

It was the incredible act of rebellion in Eden against the Almighty that separated man from his Creator. No less astonishing is the fact that man continues his defiance in his very attempts to be reconciled to God, and so persists in his self-righteous resolve to contribute something toward his salvation.

Thus, amazingly, man's rebellion against God is seen most clearly in his religions, all of which are but mirror images of Babel—ingenious and persistent attempts to "climb up some other way" instead of entering through the door which God has provided in His Son (John 10:9).

Babel may be traced through ancient paganism to the "high places" (elevated altars) of heathen worship adopted by Israel (Leviticus 26:30; 1 Kings 11:7; 2 Kings 23:15; Ezekiel 16:24-39) and to every religion on earth today. The ornate temples, mosques, and elaborate ceremonies found in Islam, Hinduism, Buddhism, Mormonism, and other cults and the occult are obvious continuations of Babel. So are the magnificent cathedrals, lofty steeples, exalted and gilded altars, luxurious vestments and impressive rituals of some of today's churches, both Protestant and Roman Catholic.

Such pomp turns off many non-Christians, who rightly want nothing to do with a God who is influenced by fleshly enhancements.

But was not Solomon's temple most magnificent? Yes, but it was uniquely designed and commanded by God. Both the tabernacle in the wilderness and the temple which succeeded it were "a figure [picture]...of good things to come [that is, of Christ and heaven]" (Hebrews 9:9-11). God said to Moses, "See...that thou make all things according to the pattern showed to thee in the mount [Sinai]" (Hebrews 8:5).

No such pattern or approval was given by God for any other religious structure. While Protestants reject relics, statues, and icons, they often refer to their places of worship as "sanctuaries," as though God dwells there. In fact, God inhabits the Christian's body ("your body is the temple of the Holy Ghost"—1 Corinthians 6:19), which is therefore to be kept holy. Paul reminded the Athenians:

> God that made the world and all things therein,
> seeing that he is Lord of heaven and earth,
> dwelleth not in temples made with hands; neither
> is worshipped with men's hands, as though he
> needed any thing, seeing he giveth to all life, and
> breath, and all things (Acts 17:24,25).

Jesus explained that God does, indeed, desire our worship—but it must be "in spirit and in truth" (John 4:23,24). Affectations, whether in physical adornments, props, or ceremonies, appeal to the flesh and, far from enhancing worship, deny both the truth and the Spirit by which it alone can be offered to the God who created and redeemed us. Sacramentalism—the belief that liturgy's form and formulas transmit spiritual power and that salvation comes through the sacraments—too readily creeps into even Protestant thinking. In fact, some still believe that baptism saves and that taking the bread and cup brings life.

Alas, we are all Eve's children by nature and still prone to follow the ways of Cain and the tower of Babel. Every place of worship which has been adorned for the purpose of hallowing it or gaining God's favor or making worship more acceptable violates Exodus 20:24-26 as well as the rest of Scripture. All such "sanctuaries" are monuments to man's rebellion and his proud and perverted religion of self-effort.

Unfortunately, it is all too easy to fall into the error of imagining that belonging to a church and periodically "worshiping" in its "sanctuary" makes one a Christian and compensates for one's lack of consistent, personal holiness.

Of course, no one in today's world is under the illusion that one can climb a physical tower to heaven. Yet the folly of today's religions is every bit as monumental, and the anarchy against God which motivates those beliefs is just as evil, as was the Tower of Babel. Billions continue, in the spirit of Babel, to pursue equally futile self-oriented religious programs to earn their way to heaven. In the process, *truth* and *doctrine* are relegated to a secondary role, or none.

Sadly, for many, faith is a power of the mind and God is merely a placebo that helps one "believe" and thereby activates this mind power. "Prayer is communicating with the deep unconscious....Your unconscious mind...[has a] power that turns wishes into realities," says a popular writer. He says further, "You don't know the power you have within you!...You make the world into anything you choose." It is Babel again in a more sophisticated form. The power of "thinking" becomes the magic stairway that leads to the paradise where all one's wishes can be fulfilled.

God has blasphemously been called "the greatest Positive Thinker that ever was!" To some "faith teachers" faith is a mind power which even God uses—a force contained in words and released when one speaks forth "the word of faith." "By the spoken word," declares one such teacher, "we create our universe...you create the presence of Jesus with your mouth...through visualization and dreaming you can incubate your future and hatch the results." Here we have an evangelical form of Christian Science or Science of Mind.

Many Christians have unwittingly believed a similar lie. They imagine that faith is believing that what they are praying for will happen. Of course, if *believing* something will happen *causes* it to happen, then who needs God? Men themselves have become gods. The power of belief becomes one's Tower of Babel, the magic steps by which one climbs to that "state of mind called heaven."

Biblical faith, however, is believing that *God* will answer one's prayer. That changes everything! We could never truly believe a prayer would be answered—nor would we want it to be—unless we were certain it was God's will. Faith is not a magic power we aim at God to get Him to bless our plans, but "the obedience of faith" (Romans 16:26) brings us into submission to Him as the instruments of His will.

Humanists also have their Babel-like, do-it-yourself religion. They call it science. It, too, reflects man's continued rebellion. Modern man hopes to conquer the atom, space, and all disease and thus become immortal master of the universe.

The materialist's "heaven" is a peaceful cosmos populated by highly evolved, space-traveling civilizations which have restored paradise through super technology.

Rank materialism leaves the soul empty, but adding a touch of religion to science seems to fill the void while keeping faith "rational." There is no more deadly delusion than a scientific religion. It is the delusion of Babel all over again, with advancing knowledge building the steps that both lead man to "heaven" and open to him the very powers of God.

One of Christian psychology's major appeals to evangelicals is its false claim to being scientific. It fails, however, the litmus test of Exodus 20:24-26. Its altars are built of the cut and polished stones of human wisdom, its rituals are not found in Scripture, and self rather than God is the object of worship. Moreover, on its altars burns the strange fire (Leviticus 10:1; Numbers 3:4) of humanistic theories unacceptable to God.

Religious science is a major element in the environmental movement, where the earth is increasingly viewed as sacred. Ecotheology, says a Georgetown University professor, "starts with the premise that the Universe is God." "If we must worship a power greater than ourselves," intones Carl Sagan, "does it not make sense to revere the Sun and stars?" To draw closer to, and thus better observe and worship, the heavenly bodies was a major purpose of the Tower of Babel.

The environmental movement, too, is a humanistic attempt to restore the lost paradise of Eden without repenting of rebellion against the Creator.

Such is the message that is being seductively presented to America's children in the public schools. New Age doctrine is being purposefully promoted in the public schools through such programs as America 2000. As governor of Arkansas, Bill Clinton initiated school reform which had much to do with remolding the students into planetary citizens alienated from parents. Former students at the "Governor's school" testify that foul language was encouraged as part of a brainwashing procedure designed to strip students of biblical morals. There was blatant promotion of gay lifestyles, free sex, rebellion, and New Age beliefs and practices, including the worship of self and of the universe as God.

Exodus 20:24-26 is a foundational passage which makes it clear that the earth is neither to be honored nor worshiped, but to be used as an altar. Sin brought a curse upon the earth, a curse which could be removed only through the shedding of blood (Leviticus 17:11). Animals were sacrificed upon an altar of earth in anticipation of the Lamb of God, who would, "by the sacrifice of himself" (Hebrews 9:26), once and for all obtain "eternal redemption for us" (verse 12).

It is for man's own good that God visits sin with death. How horrible it would be for mankind to continue forever in its state of rebellion, thus perpetuating ever increasing evil, sickness, suffering, sorrow, and death. Only out of death in payment of the full penalty for sin comes resurrection (not reincarnation's amoral recycling of evil) and a whole new universe into which sin and suffering can never enter.

Such is God's desire and provision for all mankind. Those who reject the free gift of eternal life offered by His grace will experience eternal regret in the tormenting finality of their endless separation from God.

The "gospel of God," as we have seen, is very specific and must be believed for one to be saved. "Strait is the gate, and narrow is the way, which leadeth unto life, and few there be that find it" (Matthew 7:14). That "narrow-minded" statement was not the invention of some dogmatic fundamentalist, but came from our Lord Himself.

"The faith" for which we must "earnestly contend" (Jude 3) has definite moral and doctrinal content and must be believed for salvation. All else is Babel.

8

The Call to Discipleship

*Go ye therefore, and [make disciples of] all
nations...teaching them to observe all things
whatsoever I have commanded you: and, lo, I am
with you alway, even unto the end of the world.*
—Matthew 28:19,20

We see from God's Word that lost sinners are offered forgiveness of all sins (past, present, and future) and eternal life
as a free gift of God's grace by virtue of Christ's fully accomplished redemptive work upon the cross and His bodily resurrection. To receive these priceless gifts one need only
believe the gospel: that one is a sinner deserving God's judgment and unable by self-effort, religious ritual, or any other
means to earn or merit salvation even in part; and that Christ
paid the full debt which God's justice demands for man's
sin. Of course, one must believe the gospel not merely as historic fact but to the extent of placing one's faith completely in
the Lord Jesus Christ as personal Savior for eternity.

Christ directed His disciples to preach the good news of
the gospel to everyone everywhere. This command to His

original followers has become known as the "Great Commission." It is stated in two ways: "go into all the world and *preach the gospel*" (Mark 16:15); and "*make disciples*" (Matthew 28:19,20 NASB). Those who preach the gospel are to disciple those who believe it. Born again by God's Spirit into His family (John 3:3-5; 1 John 3:2), converts begin a new life as Christ's followers, eager to learn of Him and to obey the One to whom they now owe such an infinite debt of gratitude.

Christ warned that some would seem to receive the gospel with great enthusiasm only to become entangled in the world, discouraged and disillusioned. They would eventually turn back from following Him. Many maintain a façade of Christianity without inward reality, deceiving perhaps even themselves. Never fully convinced in their hearts, they are unwilling nevertheless to admit their unbelief. "Examine yourselves," Paul warned, "whether ye be in the faith" (2 Corinthians 13:5).

Of those who are genuine, all too few are able to give a reason for the hope that is in them (1 Peter 3:15). How many Christians are able to convincingly persuade an atheist, Buddhist, Hindu, Muslim, or New Ager with overwhelming evidence and sound reason from Scripture? God's Word is the sword of the Spirit, but few know it well enough to quell their own doubts, much less to convert others.

> At the heart of Christ's call to discipleship is the daily application of His cross in each life.

One of today's greatest needs is for solid Bible teaching that produces disciples who are able to "earnestly contend for the faith once [for all] delivered to the saints" (Jude 3). That faith for which we must contend was delivered by Christ to the original twelve disciples, who were then to teach those whom they evangelized "*to observe all things*" that Christ had commanded them.

Through succeeding generations of those who have been won to Him and who have in turn, in obedience to their Lord, discipled others, this unbroken chain of command comes down to us in our time. Not some special priest or clergy class, but each Christian today, like those who have passed before, is a successor to the apostles. Think of what that means!

At the heart of Christ's call to discipleship is the daily application of His cross in each life. Yet one seldom hears in evangelical circles Christ's definitive declaration: "And whosoever doth not bear his cross, and come after me...[and] forsaketh not all that he hath, he cannot be my disciple" (Luke 14:27-33). The call to discipleship must be honestly faced. Through the cross we die to self and begin to live to our Lord in resurrection power (Galatians 2:20). Indeed, Christ's death on the cross would have been a hollow act if it did not bring forth new life, for now and for eternity.

Resurrection life reckons the old life dead and makes no provision for the flesh (Romans 6:4,11; 13:14). Instead of the popular self-esteem, God calls us to deny self, to love truth and hate folly, to please God instead of others or ourselves, no matter what the cost in this life. Never mind social pressures from what others think, say, or do. We must be fully persuaded that what God thinks and what He will say when we appear before Him one day is all that matters.

As Jim Elliot, one of the five martyrs killed in Ecuador in 1956, said when as a young man he chose the mission field over more popular careers, "He is no fool who gives up what he cannot keep to gain what he cannot lose." That choice is only logical if one believes that time is short and eternity is endless. Such commitment brings heavenly joy, peace, and a fulfillment that nothing earth offers can rival.

To those whom He called into a saving relationship with Himself, Christ said, "Follow me" (Matthew 4:19; 8:22; 9:9; 16:24). This simple command, which our Lord repeated after His resurrection (John 21:19,22) is as applicable to Christians today as it was when He called the first disciples.

What does it mean to follow Christ? Did He promise His followers that they would be successful, wealthy, and esteemed in this world?

God may grant earthly success to a few for His own purposes. On the whole, however, our Lord declared that those who were true to Him would follow in His path of rejection and suffering: "If the world hate you, ye know that it hated me before it hated you....The servant is not greater than his lord. If they have persecuted me, they will also persecute you...for my name's sake..." (John 15:18-21).

Such was the lot of the early church. Yet today Christianity is popularized as the key to "the good life." We try to attract youth to Christ by persuading them that it's "cool" to be a Christian. The idea of suffering for Christ doesn't suit a worldly church. How strange such verses as the following seem to Christians in America: "For unto you it is given in the behalf of Christ, not only to believe on him, but also to suffer for his sake" (Philippians 1:29). Suffering is *given* to us? Paul speaks as though it were a precious privilege to suffer for His sake. After being imprisoned and beaten, the early disciples rejoiced "that they were counted worthy to suffer shame for his name" (Acts 5:41). Such is the commitment to which the gospel actually calls us.

Christ told His disciples after His resurrection, "As my Father hath sent me, even so send I you" (John 20:21). The Father sent the Son as a lamb to the slaughter into a world that would hate and crucify Him. And as the Father sent Him, so Christ sends us into a world that He promises will treat His followers as it did Him. Are we willing? Is this your idea of Christianity? If not, then think again and check it out against the Scriptures. Today's popularized "Christianity" is further from Him and His truth than we realize.

Peter, who failed so miserably and was restored by the Lord, explained that Christians would be hated, falsely accused, and persecuted, and were expected to suffer these wrongs patiently (1 Peter 2:19,20; 4:12-19). Under the inspiration of the Holy Spirit he wrote, "For even hereunto were ye called: because Christ also suffered for us, leaving us an example, that ye should follow his steps: who did no sin, neither was guile found in his mouth: who, when he was reviled, reviled not again; when he suffered, he threatened not, but committed himself to him that judgeth righteously: who his own self bare our sins in his own body on the tree, that we, being dead to sins, should live unto righteousness..." (1 Peter 2:21-25).

Christians are being imprisoned and martyred again in communist China and in some Muslim countries. Similar persecutions could well overtake us in America.

Recently I listened with tears welling in my eyes as my wife, Ruth, read to me some of the history of her ancestors. For being rebaptized after they became Christians (and thus denying the efficacy of Rome's infant baptism), many of these Anabaptists were burned at the stake. To escape the flames many others fled the Inquisition in Holland to Prussia. From there they fled to Russia, and in the closing days of World War II many attempted an escape from godless and oppressive communism back to the West.

Out of one group of 611 leaving Russia, only 31 arrived back in Holland. Tramping day and night through the snow, unable to find food or shelter, some were caught and returned. Others were killed or died of exposure. Children were torn from parents, husbands from wives. The terror and agony were beyond imagination. Yet those who survived came through with their faith not only intact but strengthened.

As Ruth read of the indescribable suffering, I thought of the thousands of Christians in America who find it necessary to enter "therapy" and spend months, if not years, dealing with comparatively trifling "hurts from the past." I thought of the thousands of Christian psychologists who encourage their clients to pity themselves, to pamper their "inner child," when what they need is to deny self, take up the cross, and follow Christ.

In contrast, I was inspired by the testimony of those who suffered the loss of possessions, of loved ones, of almost every earthly hope and joy, yet triumphed through their faith in Christ. Going to a "therapist" and engaging in self-pity would have seemed incomprehensible to them when they had the Lord and His Word and when they knew that "our light affliction, which is but for a moment, worketh for us a far more exceeding and eternal weight of glory" (2 Corinthians 4:17).

> "As ye have therefore received Christ Jesus the Lord, so walk ye in him."
> —Colossians 2:6

Whence comes the strength to stand against over-whelming suffering and to triumph as Christ's faithful disciples? Oddly enough, victory comes not through our strength but through our weakness.

When Paul cried out for deliverance from a severe trial, Christ replied that He had allowed it to make Paul weak enough so that he would trust only in the Lord, rather than in his great abilities. "[M]y strength is made perfect in your weakness," our Lord promised (2 Corinthians 12:9).

Paul exhorts us, "As ye have therefore received Christ Jesus the Lord, so walk ye in him" (Colossians 2:6). Did we not receive Christ in weakness as helpless, hopeless sinners crying out to Him for mercy and grace? That, then, is the way we are to walk this path of triumph in suffering—as sinners saved by grace, weak and helpless in ourselves and trusting totally in Him.

We are earthen vessels, but we contain a great treasure: "that the excellency of the power may be of God and not of us" (2 Corinthians 4:7). Such is the secret of our triumph over the world, the flesh, and the devil. The load is too heavy for us to carry. What a relief to turn it over to Him! And what a joy to be delivered from the fear of man, from seeking to win the acclaim of this world, from seeking anything but His "well done, thou good and faithful servant" (Matthew 25:21) in that coming day.

Some manage to amass a fortune to leave at death to their heirs. Others have little of this earth's goods but have great and eternal riches laid up in heaven. It takes little wisdom to know who of these have made the wisest choice and who have been truly successful.

God has an eternal purpose for our lives. Our passion should be to know and to fulfill that purpose, beginning here on this earth. One day very soon we will each stand before Him. What a tragedy to miss the very purpose for which we were created and redeemed!

You may say, "Yes, I want to be used of God, but I don't know what He wants me to do." Or, "I try to serve Him, try to witness for Him, and it all seems to come to nothing."

Learn this: Greater than anything God can do *through* you is what He wants to do *in* you. What counts most is not quantity but quality, not so much your outward effort but your motive within—the purity of your heart rather than your prominence with men.

Moreover, what seems much in time may be very little in eternity. It is not one's talents or energy but the empowering of the Holy Spirit that produces genuine and lasting results: "Not by might, nor by power, but by my spirit, saith the Lord of hosts" (Zechariah 4:6). Trust God for the filling and empowering of His Spirit.

Millions have laid down their lives for the faith. Their commitment to Christ meant so much that they would not compromise when threatened with the most excruciating torture and death. Can we fathom their choice?

The martyrs could have chosen the ecumenical path of compromise, of avoiding controversy and affirming the "common beliefs of all religions," and thus have escaped the flame or the sword. They chose instead to stand firm for the truth, to contend earnestly for the faith.

Christ calls us to do the same.

Paul said he had been "put in trust with the gospel" (1 Thessalonians 2:4). So have each of us if we are truly Christians. Let us be certain that we keep that trust for the sake of the lost and in honor of our Lord, who paid such a price for our redemption!

There is no escaping the eternal choice which confronts us. Will we follow from afar, or will we seek to follow in our Lord's very footsteps? One day we will give an account before God for the path we choose. What joy there is now and will be eternally in being true to Him.

9

What Is the
Christian Life?

The just shall live by faith.
—HABAKKUK 2:4; ROMANS 1:17;
GALATIANS 3:11; HEBREWS 10:38

Surely a phrase that is repeated four times in the Bible must contain one of God's most important teachings. The life God gives is only for the *just*—but who is *just?* The Bible leaves no doubt as to the answer: "For there is not a just man upon earth, that doeth good, and sinneth not" (Ecclesiastes 7:20); "For all have sinned, and come short of the glory of God" (Romans 3:23). God's law demands, "Thou shalt love the Lord thy God with all thy heart, and with all thy soul, and with all thy strength, and with all thy mind; and thy neighbor as thyself" (Luke 10:27). By that standard we have all broken God's law repeatedly and are condemned.

Nor is there any way that we, as sinners, could become *just.* Living a perfect life in the future (even if that were possible) could never merit forgiveness for sins already committed or deliver from the judgment which God's justice righteously demands. Saving a million lives in the future, for example, could never atone for having taken just one life in the past. Only God could declare a sinner to be "just"—but how could He, when His irrevocable law condemns us? For God simply to forgive the sinner would violate His own law and in itself would be unjust.

Paul, inspired of the Holy Spirit, explains how God can justly justify sinners: "Being justified freely by his [God's] grace through the redemption that is in Christ Jesus; whom God hath set forth to be a propitiation through faith in his blood...for the remission of sins...that he [God] might be just, and the justifier of him which believeth in Jesus" (Romans 3:24-26). Forgiving the sinner and declaring him just comes only on the basis of Christ having paid the full penalty demanded by God's justice against sin, and the sinner having personally accepted that payment by Christ. Forgiveness cannot come about through good deeds, church attendance, sacraments, baptism, scapulars or medals, prayers, tears, promises, charitable gifts—or anything else that pastor, priest, church, or Mary could do. Only the infinite God Himself, coming as a sinless man through the virgin birth, could bear, in our place, the infinite penalty we deserved.

One cannot even begin to "live by faith" while "dead in trespasses and sins" (Ephesians 2:1), which is mankind's natural condition. One must be made "alive from the dead" (Romans 6:13) by receiving God's forgiveness in Christ. The Christian life of faith is only for those who are "in the faith" (2 Corinthians 13:5). Living "a good Christian life" is not the way to become a Christian. Only those who already are Christians can live that life. Nor is it lived in order to earn heaven, which is impossible, but out of gratitude to Christ for having paid the penalty for sin.

> The Christian life is miraculous. Expect it to be.

A Christian has been "born again" of the Spirit of God (John 3:3-8) through "the Word of God" (1 Peter 1:23) by believing the gospel (Romans 1:16) and is a "new creature" (2 Corinthians 5:17) in Christ, having been "created in Christ Jesus unto good works, which God hath before ordained that we should walk in them" (Ephesians 2:10). If we trust Him to do so, surely God will open the right doors, guide each step of every Christian's life, and provide the means of fulfilling the "good works" which He has ordained for each of us.

Clearly, one must first enter upon the Christian life by faith in Christ in order to begin to "live by faith." Paul exhorts us, "As ye have therefore received Christ Jesus the Lord, so walk ye in him" (Colossians 2:6). And how did we receive Christ? As helpless, hopeless sinners who could do nothing for our own salvation but had to look entirely to Christ to save us. In that same attitude of unworthiness and complete dependence upon God for His grace and upon Christ to live His life through us, we live by faith the Christian life.

Christ told Paul that His strength was perfected in Paul's weakness (2 Corinthians 12:9). We must stop trying to be strong in ourselves, and "be strong in the Lord, and in the power of his might" (Ephesians 6:10). The battle with the forces of evil, God assures us, will be won "not by might, nor by power, but by my spirit..." (Zechariah 4:6). There is great joy, even in great trials, in trusting Christ and seeing what He can do.

That the Christian life is to be lived by faith tells us that it comes supernaturally, not naturally, as we trust God and know and obey His Word. It cannot be by our own direction and strength but only under the leading and by the power of God, who alone is the proper object of faith. Yes, the Christian life is miraculous. Expect it to be. Beware, however, of the widespread unbiblical emphasis upon, and insatiable desire for, the miraculous, which foster delusion. One of today's most prominent televangelists and proponents of signs and wonders has written, "you can perform miracles if you but understand...the laws...that unlock God's power... the flow of God's energy...." In another book, he asserts,

"We speak to money, and it comes. We speak to storms, and they cease...." Money comes from his mailing list, and this country has recently experienced the worst storms in years without any intervention from him.

The most powerful evidence of God's supernatural work in our lives is found in the transformation of our character to Christlikeness. The "fruit," not of "therapy," but "of the Spirit," is "love, joy, peace, longsuffering, gentleness, goodness, faith, meekness, temperance" (Galatians 5:22,23). The "works of the flesh" (Galatians 5:19-21), no matter how exemplary, are not acceptable to God (Romans 8:8). To live the Christian life, one must learn to "live in the Spirit" and "walk in the Spirit" (Galatians 5:25).

This is not to deny the benefit of education, diligence, hard work, prudent investment, experience, and sound practice in earning one's "daily bread" (Matthew 6:11). Earthly success, however, though legitimate, is not the Christian's goal in life. Christ declared, "...a man's life consisteth not in the abundance of the things which he possesseth" (Luke 12:15); "Lay not up for yourselves treasures upon earth...but lay up for yourselves treasures in heaven...for where your treasure is, there will your heart be also" (Matthew 6:19-21).

> The Christian life is too glorious to be easy.

The fact that the Christian life is supernatural does not guarantee the "financial success" promised by today's false prophets—nor that we will be free of trouble, sorrow, or pain. Positive confession leaders forget that it was from *prison* that Paul wrote, "I can do all things through Christ which strengtheneth me" (Philippians 4:13); and in the same context he declared, "I have learned, in whatsoever state I am, therewith to be content" (verse 11).

The Christian life is too glorious to be easy. It *must* involve trials and testings. This was true of Christ Himself as well as of the apostles and early church. Jesus said, "In the world ye shall have tribulation" (John 16:33); "The servant is not greater than his lord. If they have persecuted me, they will also persecute you" (15:20).

Avoiding this uncomfortable truth, a "user-friendly gospel" is preached by thousands of pastors. Megachurches are created by offering an appealing "Christianity" that is guaranteed to bring success and popularity with the world, but which would not be recognized by Paul or the other apostles as the Christian life they knew. Celebrities popular with the world are paid to enter today's pulpits to endorse Christ; thereby they entice multitudes into a false Christianity. Once upon a time the Christian's heroes were missionaries and martyrs. Not today. Believers and the world now share the same role models. Today's successful church offers a Christianity guaranteed to be comfortable and which provides numerous services, from 12-step programs to psychological counseling, to escape every possible trial.

The faith by which the Christian life is to be lived and which is described as "more precious than gold" *must* be tested by temptations, trials, and difficulties. Why? So that when the faith by which the just live comes through the fire of adversity it will "be found unto praise and honour and glory at the appearing of Jesus Christ" (1 Peter 1:7). Of Christ, who left us "an example, that ye should follow his steps" (1 Peter 2:21), it was said, "who for the joy that was set before him endured the cross..." (Hebrews 12:2). We are able to endure earthly trials because our hope lies beyond this brief life: "Our light affliction, which is but for a moment, worketh for us a far more exceeding and eternal weight of glory" (2 Corinthians 4:17).

Those who have trusted God through a deep trial testify that their faith has been strengthened and their joy increased. Having to depend totally on Christ draws us closer to Him and increases our love for Him. Any counsel, help, or support we offer to those in distress should bring them through the trial of faith with their roots deepened in Christ (Isaiah 43:2), rather than enable them to escape the very challenges God intends and the work He desires to effect in their hearts.

By allowing us to face seemingly hopeless situations, God intends to move us from mere intellectual belief to practical trust in His provision.

In *The Power of the Spirit* William Law writes, "Whenever a man allows himself to have anxieties, fears, or complaints, he must consider his behavior as either a denial of the wisdom of God or as a confession that he is out of His will" (pp. 20,21). Many who call themselves Christians say they have trusted Christ with their eternal destiny, but seem unable to trust Him in this life—a fact which casts doubt on their relationship to Him.

God wants to test our faith now—and for good reason. Moses told the Israelites, "The LORD thy God led thee these forty years in the wilderness, to humble thee, and to prove thee, to know what was in thine heart, whether thou wouldest keep his commandments, or no" (Deuteronomy 8:2). Oswald Chambers said, "God wants you to understand that it is a life of *faith*, not a life of sentimental enjoyment of His blessings....Faith by its very nature must be tried.... 'Though he slay me, yet will I trust him'—this is the most sublime utterance of faith in the whole of the Bible" (*My Utmost for His Highest*, p. 305).

"Yea, though I walk *through* the valley of the shadow of death, I will fear no evil: for thou art with me," wrote David (Psalm 23:4). He did not expect, much less plead, to be given another path that would bypass that terrible valley, but only that God would be with him through his trial. Living by faith involves confronting the difficulties of life, which indeed may have been allowed of God to test and correct us. The Christian life includes learning where we have gone astray and being willing to be corrected and brought back into obedience to God and His Word. It is often in times of distress alone that God can break the hold of that which has drawn our affection away from Him, perhaps without our even knowing it.

As we walk by faith, and experience God's faithfulness in trials, praise and worship well up within us. Indeed, praise and worship are to play a significant role in the Christian life. Sadly, so many of today's praise and worship songs reflect the lack of depth in current Christianity. Congregational singing often consists of empty, repetitive choruses which have taken the place of the old hymns of the faith. Phrases are repeated again and again, such as "We worship You, Lord, we praise You, Lord, we lift Your name on high, we lift our hands, we exalt You," and so on. There is much clapping and swaying to the catchy tune and beat. Yet the congregation and the "worship team" seem oblivious of the fact that instead of truly praising and worshiping, they are merely singing words about praise and worship, without mentioning God's character, qualities, and deeds which evoke worship.

Sound doctrine, too, plays a vital role in the Christian life of faith. Paul's life sets the example for us all. In describing his life to Timothy, he put *doctrine* first: "But thou hast fully known my doctrine, manner of life, purpose, faith, longsuffering, charity, patience, persecutions, afflictions....Yea, and all that will live godly in Christ Jesus shall suffer persecution" (2 Timothy 3:10-12). He also warned that "the time will come when they will not endure sound doctrine" (4:3). We are in that day. Doctrine is despised. Entertainment and sermonettes are more popular with today's Christianettes.

One well-known Christian leader writes that "the Bible is not an impractical book of theology, but rather a practical book of life containing a system of thought and conduct that will guarantee success...." His idea that theology is "impractical" is shared by millions. And "success"—which he, as a multimillionaire, enjoys in abundance—is now measured by the world's standards instead of by God's.

Our hope is in heaven and in the imminency of the rapture which will transport us out of this evil world into His presence. In the meantime, our confident trust in our Lord through the trials of this life of faith demonstrates the reality of our trust in Him for eternity. A true story about Blondin, who walked back and forth on a tightrope across Niagara Falls, illustrates the point.

One day, in the crowd watching Blondin, a spectator was trying to explain to a younger man what it means to truly trust Christ. "What do you think of Blondin?" he asked. "He's the greatest!" came the enthusiastic response. "Do you think he can carry a man across and back?" "Of course," was the immediate reply. "I've seen him do it." Looking the younger man squarely in the eye, the questioner said, "When Blondin comes back from the other side, he's going to call for a volunteer. Will you be the man?" The young man turned white. "Not on your life!" he exclaimed.

Many have a similarly theoretical faith in Christ. They can sing enthusiastically about salvation, but when life's adversities strike they have no real peace and joy and run to the nearest therapist instead of to the Lord. May He give us grace to live by faith as true Christians; and may earth's trials strengthen our faith, deepen our love for God, increase our fellowship with and joy in Him, and bring honor and glory to Him for eternity.

10

The Sufficiency
of Scripture

*All scripture is given by inspiration of God,
and is profitable for doctrine, for reproof, for
correction, for instruction in righteousness:
That the man of God may be perfect, thoroughly
furnished unto all good works.*
—2 TIMOTHY 3:16,17

How it strengthens our faith and rejoices our hearts to read the testimonies of the Holy Spirit-inspired writers of Scripture who found the Bible sufficient for their every need. And how sad it is in our day to find Christian leaders teaching that the Bible is deficient for modern man and needs to be supplemented by humanistic myths. For encouragement in the faith, consider again what the writers of the Old and New Testaments had to say about the sufficiency and perfection of God's Holy Word. It says

> Psalm 1 makes it clear that those who obey, delight in, and meditate upon God's Word day and night will flourish like trees growing beside a river.

therein that God has given to us *"all* things that pertain unto
life and godliness" (2 Peter 1:3,4).

Psalm 1 makes it clear that those who obey, delight in, and
meditate upon God's Word day and night will flourish like
trees growing beside a river. Their Holy Spirit-empowered
lives will produce fruit for God in abundance and perfection—without any help from the philosophies of men. In
Psalm 19 David exults, "The law of the Lord is perfect, con-
verting the soul: the testimony of the Lord is sure, making
wise the simple. The statutes of the Lord are right, rejoicing
the heart...More to be desired are they than gold...sweeter
also than honey...and in keeping of them there is great
reward" (verses 7-11). Psalm 119 declares, "Wherewithal shall
a young man cleanse his way? By taking heed thereto
according to thy word...O how love I thy law! It is my meditation all the day. Thou through thy commandments hast
made me wiser than mine enemies...I have more understanding than all my teachers...I understand more than the
ancients, because I keep thy precepts...Thy word is a lamp
unto my feet and a light unto my path" (verses 9,97-100,105).
Examples could be multiplied of those who found God's
Word not only sufficient but "the joy and rejoicing of mine
heart" (Jeremiah 15:16). How much more should we.

The sufficiency and importance of biblical truth and doctrine are presented powerfully in John's brief second epistle.
John mentions *truth* five times in the first four verses. He then
warns about deceivers who pose as Christians but who deny
the *doctrine of Christ.* Showing how essential sound doctrine
is, he declares that anyone who "abideth not in the doctrine of
Christ, hath not God" (verse 9). He then commands separation from such persons. How important, then, is the current
battle being waged for sound doctrine.

Most of the epistles were written to correct doctrinal
error. Doctrinal purity is essential not only for salvation but
also for living the Christian life. Paul wrote to Timothy,
"Thou has fully known my *doctrine,* manner of life, purpose,

faith, longsuffering, charity, patience, persecutions, afflictions...." (2 Timothy 3:10,11). Doctrine was the very foundation of Paul's life. And so it must be of ours.

Universalisms, such as "anyone can worship God in his own way," are condemned by John's statement that "Whosoever transgresseth, and abideth not in the doctrine of Christ, hath not God" (2 John 9). Why? Because Christ said, "I am the way, the truth, and the life: no man cometh to the Father, but by me" (John 14:6). This statement is foundational to the "doctrine of Christ" that John says separates true Christians from the rest of the world. In defense of that doctrine, millions have died as martyrs of the faith.

Truth is the issue, and it both unites and divides. It unites those committed to it, and at the same time divides them from all others who oppose sound doctrine. It is bad enough to propose "unity" between fundamentalism and modernism, Protestantism and Catholicism. The ecumenism of "Christian psychology," however, that attempts to unite theology with psychology, the evangelical faith with the teachings of godless humanists, is equally bad.

No evangelical would interpret "I am the way" to mean that Christ is only one of many ways to God; or "I am the life" to mean that the life He is and offers needs to be supplemented from other sources. To do so would be a complete denial of the *doctrine of Christ*. Nor can His statement, "I am the truth," be interpreted to mean that He is only part of the truth. Yet this is the pernicious effect of "Christian psychology's" specious slogan, "all truth is God's truth." No longer Christ and His Word alone, but now Freud and others are also legitimate sources of "God's truth." There is no reason, then, why Mary Baker Eddy, Buddha, and the Hindu Vedas may not also be accepted as sources of "God's truth." This heresy is so persistent that I make no apology for dealing with it repeatedly.

The "all truth is God's truth" euphemism is a basic denial of the *doctrine of Christ*, which declares that Christ is *the truth*. God's truth is "as the truth is in Jesus" (Ephesians 4:21).

Christ the Living Word is revealed in the written Word: "Sanctify them through thy truth: thy word is truth" (John 17:17). Christ did not say, "If ye continue in my word...ye shall know part of the truth and you shall be made partially free. There is more truth yet to be revealed through godless humanists that will liberate future generations more completely than I can now free you through my Word and my Spirit alone." Yet that is the teaching of "Christian psychology." In *Can You Trust Psychology* Gary Collins writes, "The Bible speaks to human needs...But God in his goodness also has allowed us [Freud, Jung, et al.] to discover psychological truths about human behavior and counseling that are never mentioned in Scripture but are consistent with the written Word of God and helpful to people facing the problems of modern living." Here is another example of subtle redefinition whereby *biblical* no longer means *derived* from God's Word, but derived elsewhere, then declared to be *consistent* with Scripture.

Those who proclaim that "all truth is God's truth" confuse *the truth* with mere *facts of nature*. That the latter are not included in the former is quite clear from what Jesus said: "When he, the Spirit of truth, is come...whom the world cannot receive...he will guide you into *all truth*" (John 16:3; 14:17; 16:13). Since all truth is revealed only by the Spirit of God "whom the world cannot receive," and since "the natural man receiveth not the things of the Spirit of God" (1 Corinthians 2:14), if science were part of "God's truth," then all scientific discoveries would have to be made only by Christians. Yet non-Christians make great scientists. So even if psychology were a science, which it is not, it would still not be part of "God's truth," which is revealed by God only to His own.

> God's truth as revealed by the Holy Spirit in His Word sets us free from sin and leads us into victorious living.

God's truth as revealed by the Holy Spirit in His Word sets us free from sin and leads us into victorious living. It has nothing to do with science, but involves the moral and spiritual part of man. As soon as science pretends to deal with spiritual truth it has overstepped its bounds. Physics, chemistry, medicine, and so on make no such pretense, but "Christian psychology" does, which is why it is so fallacious and dangerous.

The *doctrine of Christ* forms the basis for a victorious life of "love, joy, peace, longsuffering, gentleness, goodness, faith, meekness, temperance" through the power of the Holy Spirit (Galatians 5:22,23). What is that doctrine? That Christ is God Himself become man to die for our sins. Resurrected and ascended on high, He comes by His Spirit to live in those who open their hearts to Him. Christ likened Himself to a vine that pours its life through us, the branches, to produce fruit in us for the Father. This dynamic union is no mere mystical experience, but is itself based upon *doctrine*, that is, what we believe and understand of "the truth as it is in Jesus." John's declaration that we must abide in the doctrine of Christ elaborates upon Christ's statement, "Abide in me" (John 15:4). As with Paul, so for us today: the lives we live must spring from the doctrine of Christ and be consistent with it.

So essential is sound doctrine that the Holy Spirit through John commands that those who "bring not this doctrine" are not to be received into our houses nor are we to "bid [them] God speed" (2 John 10). This does not mean that we may not invite Jehovah's Witnesses or Mormons who knock on our doors to come into our homes for a discussion. However, we must do so only to *evangelize* them, making it clear that we oppose their false teachings. This must be our consistent stance toward all who deny the doctrine of Christ, even though they pass for Christian leaders in today's church.

Can't we "just love people" and "accept them" for who they are? In fact it is because we love them that we point out their error and seek to correct them. Our Lord said, "As many as I love, I rebuke and chasten: be zealous therefore, and repent" (Revelation 3:19). Love is not an undiscriminating acceptance of false teachers. John writes, "This is love, that we walk after his commandments" (2 John 6), and that involves standing firm for the doctrine of Christ. The whole purpose of Christ's coming was not to "accept us as we were" but to rescue us from what we were and to change us into what He desires us to become. If Christ is truly dwelling in us, then we will yearn for that same transformation in those to whom we "[speak] the truth in love" (Ephesians 4:15).

11

All the Counsel of God

*I kept back nothing that was profitable
unto you....Wherefore I take you to record this
day, that I am pure from the blood of all men.
For I have not shunned to declare unto
you all the counsel of God.*
—ACTS 20:20,26,27

By "profitable," Paul did not mean monetarily advantageous, but all that is necessary and helpful for a joyful, fruitful, and triumphant Christian life whenever and wherever lived. How encouraging, comforting, and inspiring it must have been to those early Christians to know that "all the counsel of God" was available to them! Surely this is exactly what we need in our time.

Logically, this declaration by Paul is a challenging rebuke of much that is called "Christianity" today. How could Paul have kept back nothing that was profitable and taught all the counsel of God, when he was ignorant of "Christian" psychology, 12-Step programs, inner healing, visualization, positive confession, seed faith, the laughing revival, the binding of territorial

> What could be more thrilling than having God Himself as one's personal Counselor and to be assured that the Bible contains all the counsel of God?

spirits, and other inventions lately considered so vital? One can only conclude that these new teachings and practices are neither profitable nor part of God's counsel.

Those who advocate teachings outside of God's counsel can hardly complain that NAMBLA (North American Man-Boy Love Association), outspoken advocate of pedophilia, was formed in a church with a number of "Christian" leaders, both Protestant and Catholic, participating and voicing their approval of this perversion. Concerned conservatives call for a "return to traditional moral values." Yes, but to what tradition and by what authority? By the mutual consent of decent society? How is that defined? We desperately need to heed the counsel of God.

What could be more thrilling than having God Himself as one's personal Counselor and to be assured that the Bible contains all the counsel of God? That perfect counsel, of course, does not offer business success or instructions in repairing an engine, flying an airplane, or operating a computer. It teaches us, as spirit beings made in the image of God (Genesis 1:27; 9:6) and living in physical bodies and redeemed by Christ's blood (Galatians 3:13; 1 Peter 1:18,19; Revelation 5:9), to glorify Him in body and in spirit (1 Corinthians 6:20) here on this earth—and prepares us to be forever in His presence.

The Bible has rightly been called "the Manufacturer's handbook." God our Maker (see Psalm 95:6; Proverbs 22:2; Isaiah 17:7) intended the creatures He made to continually consult that handbook in faith. Surely our Maker included in His operating manual every instruction needed for His creatures to function holily (Leviticus 11:44,45; 19:2; 1 Thessalonians 2:10), happily (Psalm 146:5; Proverbs 3:13,18; 16:20; John 13:17), and fruitfully (Genesis 1:28; John 15:4,8;

Colossians 1:10). Surely God has not overlooked any possible problem or malfunction which might befall us nor failed to provide complete instructions and all appropriate remedies.

Suppose the descendants of Adam become angry, frustrated, fearful, anxious, insecure, lonely; or suppose they feel misused and abused or useless and lacking in purpose or meaning. Let them turn for counsel and help to their Maker, who knows everything about them, and to the Manufacturer's handbook in which He has provided complete operating instructions. As David said, "What time I am afraid, I will trust in thee" (Psalm 56:3). Let them turn to Christ, who indwells and empowers and whose very name is Counselor (Isaiah 9:6). What further counsel or help could they need?

Indeed, until very recently the people of God looked to Him alone for their spiritual and emotional needs—and triumphed by faith. Consider the suffering Job endured without any counseling or therapy from a Christian psychologist. If he didn't need it, then surely those who suffer far less don't need this newly invented help today. Job's trials and the remedy he found through trust in God and submission to His will teach us that trials must be endured for our own good, to refine and mature us; and that God Himself will be with us and is all we need to carry us through.

Or consider Joseph. Misunderstood and criticized by his parents and hated by his brethren, who wanted to kill him, he was sold into Egypt. There he was falsely accused and wrongly imprisoned, and left to languish as a criminal. How could he have survived with no psychological counseling, 12-Step programs, or inner healing to provide the help that so many now consider to be essential? In fact, he triumphed gloriously! Logically, then, if today's new remedies weren't needed by Joseph, they aren't needed now.

Compare anyone's suffering today with what Paul endured: "In labours more abundant, in stripes [scourgings] above measure, in prisons more frequent, in deaths oft. Of the Jews five times received I [39] stripes...[40 lashes were often fatal]. Thrice was I beaten with rods, once was I stoned, thrice I suffered shipwreck, a night and a day I have been in the deep; in journeyings often, in perils of waters, in perils of robbers, in perils by mine own countrymen, in perils by the heathen, in perils in the city, in perils in the wilderness, in perils in the sea, in perils among false brethren; in weariness and painfulness...hunger and thirst, in fastings often, in cold and nakedness...[and] that which cometh upon me daily, the care of all the churches" (2 Corinthians 11:23-28).

Of course it was Paul's sense of self-worth, his positive self-image, and his high self-esteem that carried him through, right? Wrong! This pitiful humanistic theory so popular in the church has proved to be so false and harmful that even much of the secular world is abandoning it. *Newsweek's* cover of February 17, 1992 announced its feature article in large letters: "The Curse of Self-Esteem: What's Wrong with the Feel Good Movement." A November 23, 1995 article by a professor/researcher in Portland, Oregon's *The Oregonian* newspaper was titled, "Note to California: Drop self-esteem, Self-control is most important...." (California, with its Self-Esteem Task Force, like leading Christian psychologists, has spent years trying to prove that self-esteem is vital, and has failed.) Based upon years of research, the author declares, "If we could cross out self-esteem and put in self-control, kids would be better off and society in general would be much better off." This is precisely what the Bible has always said. Yet this fallacious and harmful theory is the very bread and butter of Christian psychology.

Paul called himself the chief of sinners (1 Timothy 1:15), considered himself "less than the least of all saints" (Ephesians 3:8), unworthy to be an apostle (1 Corinthians 15:9), and rejoiced in his weakness. Yet he claimed to be able to do "*all things* through Christ" (Philippians 4:13) and to be always victorious (1 Corinthians 15:57; 2 Corinthians 2:14; Philippians 1:20). Christ told Paul, "My grace is sufficient for thee: for my strength is made perfect in [your] weakness." Paul's response? "Most gladly therefore...that the power of

Christ may rest upon me....I take pleasure in...persecutions, in distresses for Christ's sake: for when I am weak, then am I strong" (2 Corinthians 12:9,10).

In contrast to Paul's joy and victory through Christ alone, many of today's Christians put their trust in Christian psychology as well. Its false theories and therapies offer new comfort to the abused, confused, and depressed, making it the fastest growing and most monetarily profitable movement in the church. It is commonly accepted among evangelicals that God's counsel in the Bible is deficient and needs to be supplemented with psychology.

We are plagued by the "yes, but" syndrome. Isn't the Bible God's inerrant Word? *Yes, but...I've tried it and it doesn't work.* Don't we have the leading of the Holy Spirit, and Christ indwelling to guide and empower us? *Yes, but...*and silence. Was not the Word of God, the comfort and guidance of the Holy Spirit, and the indwelling Christ enough for suffering and martyred Christians during the first nineteen centuries of the church? *Yes, but...the world is more complex today and we need additional help.* The heroes and heroines of the faith mentioned in Hebrews 11 triumphed amidst fierce persecution without psychology. *Yes, but...you don't understand my situation...my children, my husband, my wife, my boss, the abuse I suffered as a child....*

The issue is very simple: Either "all the counsel of God" is sufficient or God has failed us. If Christian psychology, inner healing, 12-Step programs, and today's other new techniques for deliverance truly have something of value to offer, then the Bible is deficient and for 1900 years God left His church without the insights and tools it needed. Who could believe that?

Like Adam and Eve, mankind still flees the voice of God, clothes itself with the makeshift garments of new theories no better than fragile leaves, and hides behind the trees of its latest excuses for unbelief and rebellion. Psychological theories come and go in a steady stream of folly. For example, *drapetomania* was the official psychiatric diagnosis of a "mental illness" that was epidemic in early America. Afflicting only slaves, it was marked by a compulsion to escape—and vanished with the Civil War.

> One must know the whole Bible and not merely favorite or "positive" parts of it.

The diagnostic and treatment record hasn't improved since. The famous Jewish psychiatrist, Thomas Szasz, called psychology "the clever and cynical destruction of the spirituality of man, and its replacement by a positivistic 'science of mind.' " He titled the book containing that statement *The Myth of Psychotherapy*. Yet the church eagerly accepts each new theory and the dependence of Christians upon unbiblical solutions continues to grow.

To encourage a passion to know and to put to use all the counsel of God is a major purpose of this book and our ministry. One must know the whole Bible and not merely favorite or "positive" parts of it. May nothing undermine our confidence that God's Word is a sufficient guide for "life and godliness" (2 Peter 1:3-9)! Only through heeding its "doctrine, reproof, correction, [and] instruction in righteousness" can we be "perfect [that is, mature, complete], thoroughly furnished unto all good works" (2 Timothy 3:16,17).

Part III

Living in the Gospel

12

Humility,
Accountability,
and Awe

For we must all appear before the
judgment seat of Christ; that every one may
receive the things done in his body...
whether...good or bad.
—2 CORINTHIANS 5:10

This writer has passed the allotted "threescore years and ten" (Psalm 90:10). The awesome reality of facing God, either through the rapture or death, confronts me with increasing impact. Often, outdoors at night, looking up at the stars and contemplating the vastness of the universe, I confess to the Lord that the thought of facing Him beyond the grave strikes fear into my heart. This fleeting life, which is "even a vapour that appeareth for a little time, and then vanisheth away" (James 4:14), will very soon have passed entirely into history with no hope of changing it. The staggering reality of eternity will encompass me.

It is not that I doubt my salvation. I have never had the slightest question about that since the night more than 60 years ago when I received Christ into my heart as my Savior and Lord. There is no fear of hell or judgment, for I believe His Word that He has paid the penalty for my sins and has given me eternal life as a free gift of His unmerited grace. I have the wonderful and absolute assurance that I will "never perish" (John 10:28)! What I fear is the awesomeness of God Himself. Who can stand in His presence?

> It is the Lord only whom we serve, seeking to follow His Word and to please Him alone.

We are such frail creatures, so pitifully blind to God's truth, so slow to learn His will and to understand His Word and ways. We have nothing of which to boast or in which to take comfort except for His grace and love. Yet we so easily forget that we are here for only a fleeting moment; we act as though this life were all there is and that it will never end. What could be greater folly?

As such thoughts overwhelm us we discover that "the fear of the Lord is the beginning of wisdom" (Proverbs 9:10). We realize at last that it is too late to play church or any other spiritual games. Gone is any interest in trying to impress anyone on this earth, whether that person be a leader of great influence or just an ordinary believer. What people think or say about us is no longer of any concern.

Yes, we must be open to valid criticism and correction that is factual and supported by God's Word—not in order to please men, but God alone. We must be careful not to be defensive of our own reputations. All that matters is God's will and glory, and what God and Christ will pronounce upon one's life in that rapidly oncoming moment of ultimate truth. This fact, together with a constant awareness of God's love and care, provide the motivation and direction for the way in which we must use our fast diminishing moments on this earth.

We neither seek the praise of men nor fear their rebuke. It is the Lord only whom we serve, seeking to follow His Word and to please Him alone. Yes, we must be the "servants of all" (Mark 10:44; Hebrews 3:5), but we do it "for the Lord's sake" (1 Peter 2:13), not "as menpleasers; but as the servants of Christ, doing the will of God from the heart" (Ephesians 6:6).

To the extent that we serve men for the rewards they offer, God is not real to us. What folly to barter away an eternal reward in exchange for anything this brief life and its temporary bankrupt tenants can offer! Even the Latin poet Juvenal, from a humanistic standpoint, wrote, "Consider it the greatest of crimes to prefer survival to honor and, out of love of physical life, to lose the very reason for living."

Christ rebuked the Pharisees with these words: "How can ye believe [be men of faith], which receive honour one of another, and seek not the honour that cometh from God only?" (John 5:44). Why can't we receive honor *both* from men and God? For a number of reasons. Christ said it is impossible "to serve two masters," especially "God and mammon [riches; that is, worldly reward]" (Matthew 6:24). Those who attempt to do so find their hearts torn and consciences dulled as the things of this life and opinions of men prove to be more real than is God Himself.

Tragically, we can be blind to the truth about our real motives because our hearts are "deceitful above all things, and desperately wicked" (Jeremiah 17:9). What Christian has not experienced praying in public and wondering within himself whether those listening realize what a great prayer is being offered! Who has not done something virtuous, kind, and seemingly selfless for the good of others and at the same time hoped that such service was noticed and admired by men? Such folly is only possible because men and their opinions loom larger than God.

If God in all of His infinite power and love were real to us, the opinions of men, either for or against us, and the honor or dishonor they may bestow would shrink into nothingness in comparison. And as God becomes real we inevitably fear Him. This is not the fear of one who is terrorized. It is a fear out of respect, the reverent awe which is becoming of us as creatures in the presence of our Creator, no matter how confident we are of His love and the acceptance we have in Christ. And is not this sense of awe too often lacking among those who gather in most churches? Are not we generally more aware of one another than of God?

We receive so many letters from Christians who are having a difficult time finding a church where the Lord is really worshiped in Spirit and in truth (John 4:24) and His Word is honored. Of course, part of the fault could lie with those who can't find a "suitable fellowship." However, the fact that this same cry is so often heard from all over the world indicates that there must be some truth in it. Who would dare to say that Christians in general and most churches are living up to the standard set forth in the New Testament? Yet we claim to study and know the New Testament, and pastors and teachers preach from it. How many of us have lost that glow of excitement and fervent love of Christ which characterized us when we were first saved? What went wrong?

One could point to a variety of causes. How many Christians spend as much time in prayer and Bible study as they do watching television? Has not television brought the world's values into our homes? Christians are to be *in* the world but not *of* the world. If we took an honest look at ourselves, would we perhaps see that many of us have become *of* the world to an extent that would alarm us if our eyes were opened to discern it? Would the rapture, if it suddenly occurred, interrupt plans and ambitions that have lowered our affection from the heavenly to the earthly?

Is it possible that somehow those of us who claim to be Christians have lost the sense of the awesomeness of God's person and presence? Could it be that church has become something we do with, and even for, one another rather than for God alone, a pattern of going together through the same routine each week which involves motions acceptable to man rather than the worship of God? Do we act as though we are in the presence of God Himself, the infinitely powerful and holy and all-knowing Creator of the universe, who holds our breath in His hand; or do we act as though we are attempting to impress and please and even entertain one another?

So what should we do? Try to "feel" the presence of God or "visualize" Him or Christ? The destructiveness of the emotionalism and occultism resulting from such techniques has been dealt with in depth both in my books and newsletter, so it will not be repeated here. Then how does God become real to us? Do we step out into nature and contemplate the wonders of His universe? That can be a legitimate part of bowing in wonder before God, which many psalms present to us (Psalm 8:3; 19:1; 104:24)—but mysticism and emotionalism can overtake us there as well. Without understanding and obeying His Word, which reveals His character and will, we would be deceived. Therein lies another problem plaguing the church: lack of discernment and accountability to God's Word.

Only the fear of the Lord will deliver us from the fear of man, from the deceit of our own hearts, and from the snare of unbiblical alliances. One often hears the naïve expression, "I embrace all those as brethren who 'love Jesus' and 'name the name of Christ.' " Yet many cultists profess to love Jesus and almost all "name the name of Christ." One must discern what is meant by such words.

Any heresy can be made to sound biblical (and even evangelical). Those who are not aware of or are too "loving" to discern its true nature are thereby deceived. For example, consider the following message placed in newspapers by the Mormon Church:

> During the Easter season we again rejoice with
> all of Christendom, and gratefully commemorate
> the resurrection of our Lord and Savior, Jesus

Christ...At this sacred season we solemnly testify that Jesus Christ is the Son of God, the Savior and Redeemer of the world. We know that He lives! We know that because He lives, we too shall live again!

How biblical it sounds! Yet terms such as "Savior" and "Redeemer" have an entirely different meaning in Mormonism from the evangelical understanding—and that fact is deliberately hidden. "Eternal life," which the Bible says is by a free gift of God's grace, is, for the Mormon, "exaltation to godhood" and comes by works and ritual. Nor are the Mormon "God" and "Jesus" at all Christian. The "God" of Mormonism is an "exalted man" with a physical body who had physical sex with Mary to produce the body Jesus needed to occupy. The Mormon "God" was once a sinful man who was redeemed by another Jesus Christ who died on the distant planet where this "God-in-the-making" lived. He eventually became a full-blown "god," like untold numbers of others before him. The Jesus of Mormonism (only one of trillions on other planets) was Lucifer's half-brother in a spirit preexistence. He was not God but came to this earth to get a body in order to become a "God." The heresy goes on and on. Obviously, this Mormon Easter ad was deceitfully designed to seem both Christian and evangelical.

> Recognizing our accountability to Him, makes us careful to follow His Word in all we say and do.

If God is real to us, so must be His Word. Recognizing our accountability to Him, that one day very soon we must stand before Him, makes us careful to follow His Word in all we say and do. Knowing that in and of ourselves we are nothing brings the humility that becomes us as frail creatures of dust. Understanding our duty to contend earnestly for the faith committed to us as His saints (Jude 3) brings boldness and unflinching purpose of heart. Humility, accountability, and awe at God's greatness: these remove all arrogance in our contending for the faith. We remember Paul's words: "If a man be overtaken in a fault, ye which are spiritual, restore such an one in the spirit of meekness; considering thyself, lest thou also be tempted" (Galatians 6:1).

13

The Commandment
to Love

Thou shalt love the Lord thy God with all thine
heart, and with all thy soul,
and with all thy might.
—Deuteronomy 6:5

The above verse perfectly defines the relationship which God intended between Himself and Israel and all mankind. Though this requirement is not explicitly stated in the Ten Commandments (Exodus 20:1-17; Deuteronomy 5:1-22), it is, according to our Lord Jesus Christ, the essence thereof, and the first and greatest commandment given by God to man (Matthew 22:35-40; Mark 12:28-31; Luke 10:25-28).

If this is the greatest commandment, then failure to love God with one's entire heart, soul, and might must be the greatest sin of which one could be guilty. Indeed, not loving God is the root of all sin. Nor is our Lord's summation of the Ten Commandments a condemnation only of atheists and pagans. It is also a

> These two commandments (to love God, then neighbor), like blossom and fruit, are inseparable.

terrible indictment of most Christians. How shamefully little love we give to God! "With all thine heart, with all thy soul, with all thy might!" said Jesus. My own conscience has been deeply convicted.

The second commandment, according to our Lord, is, "Thou shalt love thy neighbor as thyself." Obedience to this command is the essential evidence of truly loving God. John reminds us, "He that loveth not his brother whom he hath seen, how can he love God whom he hath not seen?" (1 John 4:20). Love of neighbor is the inevitable result of loving God. These two commandments (to love God, then neighbor), like blossom and fruit, are inseparable. There cannot be one without the other. Moreover, "On these two commandments," said Jesus, "hang all the law and the prophets" (Matthew 22:40). Here is the essence of all Scripture and of God's requirements for mankind.

Were it not for God's grace and the redemptive work of Christ, this clear teaching from Scripture would hang over us like a death sentence. We have disobeyed the first and greatest commandment, and as a result could not keep the second. The penalty for sin is death—eternal separation from God and from the life and love which is in Him alone. How desperately we need a Savior! And, oh, how God's gracious and complete provision in Christ should create in our hearts the very love for Him that He longs for from us!

The church is busy with conferences, conventions, seminars, and workshops where numerous subjects from healing to holiness, from prosperity to prophecy, from miracles to marriage counseling, are taught and discussed. Yet the subject of loving God is too often conspicuous by its absence. Instead, there is much emphasis upon loving self—a teaching unknown in the church until the recent advent of Christian psychology.

Jesus said, "On these two commandments [*first*, loving God; *second*, loving neighbor] hang all the law and the prophets" (Matthew 22:40). Since these two commandments are the essence of Scripture, nothing further need be nor can be added. Yet to these two has lately been added a third: the love of self. Moreover, this newly introduced "law" is declared to be the first commandment and key to all else. It is now widely taught that self-love is the great need, that we cannot fully love either God or neighbor until we first of all learn to love ourselves.

The preeminence of loving self began to be promoted fifty years ago by Erich Fromm, a blatantly anti-Christian humanistic psychologist who believed in man's innate goodness. He dared to say that Jesus taught we must first love ourselves before we can love others when He said, "Thou shalt love thy neighbor as thyself" (Matthew 19:19). Other humanistic psychologists such as Abraham Maslow and Carl Rogers picked up Fromm's concept of self-love and popularized it.

In fact, far from teaching self-love, Christ was rebuking it in the statement quoted above. He was saying, "You feed and clothe and care for yourselves day and night. Now give to your neighbors some of that attention that you lavish upon yourselves. Love your neighbor as you excessively love yourselves." Such had been the Christian understanding of this verse throughout history. Christ would hardly tell us to love our neighbors as we love ourselves if we did not already love ourselves enough. But Fromm's perverted interpretation, through Christian psychology, gained an entrance into the church.

In 1900 years no Christian author or preacher had ever discovered a single verse in the Bible that taught self-love and self-esteem. Calvin, Luther, Wesley, Spurgeon, Moody, and others found just the opposite: the necessity to deny self and to esteem others better than ourselves (Philippians 2:3). Nevertheless, humanistic psychology's emphasis upon loving self inspired Christian psychologists with a new interpretation of Scripture that seemed to support their new profession. Bruce Narramore wrote, "Under the influence of humanistic psychologists like Carl Rogers and Abraham Maslow, many of us Christians [psychologists] have begun to see our need for self-love and self-esteem. This is a good and necessary focus."

Tragically, this humanistic influence has corrupted Bible interpretation so that the lie of self-love now emanates confidently as the new truth from puplit and Christian media through pastors, preachers, teachers, and televangelists almost everywhere. The sad corollary is that the essential love of God is neglected and self-love is made preeminent. No longer are we being convicted of our failure to love God with our whole heart, soul, and might as the gravest of sins and the root of all personal problems. Instead, we are told that our problem has been a poor self-image and lack of self-love, and we are being urged to focus upon loving and esteeming and valuing ourselves. What a deadly perversion of Scripture!

There is a growing emphasis today upon world evangelism, and surely that is needful and commendable. We ought to obey the Great Commission given to us by Christ. There is also an awakening social conscience, a concern to demonstrate practical Christianity in caring for those around us, from the unborn threatened with abortion to the homeless and deprived. And so it should be. Yet that which must come first—a deep love of God—is largely forgotten.

"Though I bestow all my goods to feed the poor, and though I give my body to be burned" (1 Corinthians 13:3) may be commendable deeds, but if they are not motivated and sanctified by an all-consuming love for God, they are of no value at all in His eyes. Have we really faced the teaching of this great love chapter? How amazing and sad that love of God is buried in the flurry of activity to serve Him. Indeed, the average Christian, while he may love much else, including even the world which he is forbidden to love, gives little serious thought to loving God.

Heaven will be the ecstatic joy of eternal and infinite love. What a taste of heaven we could have now—and at the same time bring satisfaction to our Lord!

Many issues of great concern legitimately occupy the attention of church leaders and their flocks. Yet the greatest commandment, and that which God desires from us above all, is scarcely mentioned, much less given the prominence it ought to have in church fellowship and individual lives. How tragic! And what an indictment of Christianity today. None of us is innocent of this great sin. My heart has been broken as I've been convicted anew of how far I fall short of keeping the essence of God's commandments. I have cried out to Him with new sorrow and longing that He would help me to love Him with my whole heart and my neighbor as myself.

> Yes, love is commanded. True love begins in the will, not in the emotions.

The Bible is filled with injunctions to love God, with explanations of why we ought to and of the benefits to be derived thereby. Here are a few examples. Look up others and meditate upon them:

> And now, Israel, what doth the Lord thy God require of thee, but to fear the Lord thy God, to walk in all his ways, and to love him, and to serve the Lord thy God with all thy heart and with all thy soul...that thou mayest live...for he is thy life, and the length of thy days (Deuteronomy 10:12; 30:6,20).

> O Lord God of heaven, the great and terrible God, that keepeth covenant and mercy for *them that love him* and observe his commandments (Nehemiah 1:5).

> All things work together for good to *them that love God* (Romans 8:28).

> Eye hath not seen, nor ear heard, neither have entered into the heart of man, the things which God hath prepared for *them that love him* (1 Corinthians 2:9).

God even tells us in Deuteronomy 13:1-3 that He allows false prophets to work signs and wonders as a test to see "whether ye love the Lord your God with all your heart and with all your soul." We live in a time of such testing. Loving God fervently will keep us from apostasy.

Yes, love is *commanded*. True love begins in the will, not in the emotions. That love is commanded seems incomprehensible even to many Christians. The world has conditioned us to believe that one "falls in love" and that love is a romantic attraction between the sexes. "Boy meets girl and falls in love" is the most popular theme of novels and movies. Yet "love" without God brings sorrow.

"Falling in love" is perceived as being helplessly swept up in a mysterious, euphoric, overpowering feeling over which one has no control and which, inevitably, loses its magic. One is thus equally helpless in "falling out of love," and thereafter "falling in love" with someone else. A commitment of the will is missing. We are commanded to love with purity—God first of all, with our whole being, and then our neighbor as at least a partial correction of our natural tendency to excessively love ourselves. Love is a *commitment to God* that demonstrates itself in human relationships.

Yes, falling in love transforms for a time those who experience this emotion. One suddenly becomes a different person. Someone else becomes more important than oneself, bringing deliverance from the slavery to self that ordinarily imprisons us all. Self no longer receives priority, but another has become the primary focus. The love and attention that once was lavished upon oneself now is given to the one who has become the object of one's love—and that brings tremendous freedom and joy. This temporary release from self-centeredness explains more than anything else the ecstasy of love—a fact which those "in love" generally fail to realize.

If loving others is so transforming, how much more so to genuinely and deeply love God. How can this come about? God is so great, so far beyond our finite ability to comprehend, that it seems impossible to know Him. And it is impossible to love a person (except with God's love) whom one doesn't know. Love is above all personal.

It is being taught in the church that the best way to get to know God is to visualize Christ, who is God manifest in the flesh. Visualization is the most powerful occult technique. Visualizing an entity, even "God" or "Christ," puts one in touch with a masquerading demon. Yet visualization is becoming more popular than ever in the church.

Denying any occult involvement, teachers of this technique declare, "Visualize Christ as your favorite artist paints Him—then talk to Him and He will respond." What a delusion to enter into a relationship with an imaginary "Christ"! Even if the picture created in the mind were absolutely accurate, which it is not, it would be like "falling in love" with a picture and imagining that it was talking back. Such behavior borders on insanity, yet it is seriously promoted by leading Christians.

It is also suggested that visualizing Bible scenes helps to understand their teaching. Such a practice is not only occult but illogical and misleading. Obviously, visualizing oneself seated among the listening multitude will not help to understand the Sermon on the Mount. Most of those in His day who saw and heard Jesus with their physical eyes and ears neither understood nor obeyed what He said. Knowing God and His Word is not aided by images, even if accurate—much less by imagining scenes for which the Bible gives insufficient data to recreate them. "Eye hath not seen nor ear heard," but God reveals Himself and His truth to our hearts "by his Spirit...because they are spiritually discerned" (1 Corinthians 2:9-14).

Images appeal to the flesh. Beauty is only skin deep. Solomon says that "charm is deceitful and beauty is vain" (Proverbs 31:30 NASB) and Peter warns against outward attractiveness and commends "the hidden man of the heart" (1 Peter 3:4). What folly to think that an image of Christ created by one's imagination helps one to know and love Him.

Love is not primarily a feeling. It is a commitment. This is the missing ingredient in much that is called love today. A genuine and lasting commitment to one another is often lacking even in Christian marriages due to worldly influence and the promotion by church leaders of loving, esteeming, accepting, and valuing *self*.

Commitment is also the missing ingredient in many a Christian's relationship with God. Rather than working up a feeling that you love God, make a commitment to Him to love and obey Him. Jesus promised, "He that hath my commandments, and keepeth them, he it is that loveth me...and I will love him, and will manifest myself to him...and my Father will love him, and we will come unto him and make our abode with him" (John 14:21-23).

We need to know God and His love in our hearts. As we seek Him in His Word and in prayer, He will reveal Himself by His Spirit. We are to love Him with our whole heart, soul, and might. May He grant us a fresh conviction of the sin of not loving Him as we ought, and may the desire to obey this first and greatest commandment become our passion. Only then will we begin to manifest that love for one another which Christ said would be the mark whereby the world would be able to recognize His true disciples—those to whom He said, "If ye love me, keep my commandments."

14

"Love the Lord Your God"

Hear, O Israel...thou shalt love the Lord thy God with all thine heart, and with all thy soul, and with all thy might.
—DEUTERONOMY 6:4,5

Jesus said...Thou shalt love the Lord thy God with all thy heart, and with all thy soul, and with all thy mind. This is the first and great commandment.
—MATTHEW 22:37,38

If a man love me, he will keep my words: and my Father will love him, and we will come unto him, and make our abode with him.
—JOHN 14:23

Both the Ten Commandments given to Israel and the moral law God has written in every conscience (Romans 2:14,15) require each of us to love God with our entire being. Such a demand is laid upon us not because God needs our

131

love, for He is infinite and lacks nothing. Nor is it because God is self-centered or proud and thus demands that we love Him above all else. He commands us to love Him with our whole heart because nothing less could save us from our incorrigible enemy, self.

This first and greatest commandment is given for our own good. God loves each of us so much that He wants to give us the greatest possible blessing: Himself.

> What greater desire could one have than knowing God?

He does not, however, force Himself upon anyone, for that would not be love. We must genuinely and earnestly desire Him. "And ye shall seek me, and find me, when ye shall search for me *with all your heart*" (Jeremiah 29:13) is the promise of God, who otherwise hides Himself (Isaiah 45:15). And again, "He is a rewarder of them that *diligently* seek him" (Hebrews 11:6).

This fervent seeking after God with the whole heart, without which no one can know Him, has always been the mark of His true followers. One of the psalmists likened his passion for God to the thirst of a deer panting for water (Psalm 42:1,2). David expressed it the same way: "O God...I seek thee: my soul thirsteth for thee..." (Psalm 63:1). What greater desire could one have than knowing God? Yet this most worthy pursuit is neglected even by Christians.

How astonishing that the infinite Creator of the universe offers Himself to such degraded creatures as ourselves. Nor is His love an impersonal cosmic force; it is intimately personal. Think of that! Such love should awaken a fervent response within us. Yet how many of us express our love to God even once a day, let alone love Him with our entire being? Sadly, even Christians are caught up instead in the forbidden love of the world (1 John 2:15) and the pursuit of its deceitful rewards.

Loving God is the first commandment because our obedience to all His other commandments must be motivated by love for Him. Moreover, since God commands us to love Him with our whole being, then our entire life—yes, everything we think and say and do—must flow from that love. Paul reminds us that even giving everything one possesses to the poor and being martyred in the flames is in vain unless motivated by love for Him.

If loving God with one's whole being is the greatest commandment, then not to do so, as we have just seen, must be the greatest sin—indeed, the root of all sin. How is it, then, that loving God, without which all else is but "sounding brass, or a tinkling cymbal" (1 Corinthians 13:1), is not even found in the course lists of our theological seminaries? How can it be that this "first and great[est] commandment" is so neglected in the church? The sad truth is that among today's evangelicals it is not loving and esteeming God but self-love and self-esteem which are presented as the pressing need.

I speak to my own heart. At times I weep that, like Martha (Luke 10:38-42), in the busyness of *serving* Christ, I give so little thought or time to *loving* Him. Oh, to be more like Mary.

How does one learn to love God without ever having seen Him (John 1:18; 1 Timothy 6:16; 1 John 4:12,20)? Obviously, there must be a reason for loving God—or anyone. Yes, *reason* and *love* do go together. Love must result from more than a physical attraction, which, in itself, can only arouse a fleshly response. In addition to the outward appeal there are the inner beauties of personality, character, integrity, and, of course, the other's love response. God loves without such reasons. Our love, even for Him, requires them. "We love him, because he first loved us" (1 John 4:19).

Our heavenly Father loves even those who make themselves His enemies, those who defy Him, reject His laws, deny His existence, and would tear Him from His throne. Christ proved that love in going to the cross to pay the penalty for all, even asking the Father to forgive those who nailed Him there (Luke 23:34). Such is the love which the Christian, too, having experienced it for himself, is to manifest through Christ living in him: "Love your enemies, bless them that curse you, do good to them that hate you, and pray for them which despitefully use you, and persecute you" (Matthew 5:44).

To love God with our whole heart and our neighbors as ourselves is not something we can produce by self-effort. Love for our fellows must be the expression of God's love in our hearts; nor can we love God except by coming to know Him as He is. A false god won't do. No one can love the "12-Step God as you conceive Him to be." That would be like loving some imaginary person. To know the true God *is* to love Him; and to know Him better is to love Him all the more.

Most of us have an all-too-shallow knowledge of God. Nor can our love for God grow except from a deepening appreciation of His love for us—an appreciation which must include two extremes: 1) God's infinite greatness; and 2) our sinful, wretched unworthiness. That He, who is so high and holy, would stoop so low to redeem unworthy sinners supremely reveals and demonstrates His love. Such an understanding is the basis of our love and gratitude in return and will be the unchanging theme of our praise throughout all eternity in His glorious presence (Revelation 5:8-14).

> The greater our appreciation of His love for us, the greater will be our love for Him.

There can be no doubt that the clearer one's vision of God becomes, the more unworthy one feels, and thus the more grateful for His grace and love. Such has always been the testimony of men and women of God. Job cried out to God, "I have heard of thee by the hearing of the ear: but now mine eye seeth thee. Wherefore I abhor [hate] myself, and repent in dust and ashes" (Job 42:5,6). Isaiah likewise lamented, "Woe is me! For I am undone; because I am a man of unclean lips, and I dwell in the midst of a people of unclean lips: for mine eyes have seen the King, the Lord of hosts" (Isaiah 6:5).

Such recognition of their sin and unworthiness did not decrease but enhanced the saints' love for God and appreciation of His grace. The more clearly we see the infinite chasm between God's glory and our sinful falling short thereof (Romans 3:23), the greater will be our appreciation of His grace and love in bridging that gulf to redeem us. And the greater our appreciation of His love for us, the greater will be our love for Him.

There is no joy that can compare to that of love exchanged. Nor is there any sorrow so deep as that of love spurned or ignored. How it must grieve our Lord that His redeemed ones love Him so little in return. That grief comes through in Scripture passages such as these: "I have nourished and brought up children, and they have rebelled against me" (Isaiah 1:2). "Can a maid forget her ornaments, or a bride her attire? Yet my people have forgotten me days without number" (Jeremiah 2:32).

Even more reprehensible than forgetfulness and neglect is the teaching of Christian psychology that God loves us because we are lovable and worth it. One leading Christian psychologist suggests that Christians repeat, "I am a lovable person." Another boasts, "The Son of God considers us of such value that He gave His life for us." If that were true, it would increase our pride and decrease our appreciation of His love and grace. In fact, the Bible teaches that God loves us because "God is love" and in spite of our unloveliness; and our love for God and our appreciation of His love and forgiveness will be in proportion to the recognition of our sin and unworthiness.

Such was the lesson Christ taught Simon the Pharisee when He was a guest in his house. Jesus told of a creditor who forgave two debtors, one who owed a vast sum and another who owed almost nothing. Then He asked Simon, "Which of them will love him [the creditor] most?" Said Simon, "I suppose...he, to whom he forgave most." "Thou hast rightly judged," replied Jesus. Then, rebuking Simon for failing even to give Him water and a towel, and commending the woman who had been washing His feet with her tears and wiping them with her hair, Christ declared pointedly, "Her sins, which are many, are forgiven; for she loved much:

but to whom little is forgiven, the same loveth little" (Luke 7:36-47).

It is both logical and biblical that the more sinful and worthless we realize we are in God's eyes, the greater our gratitude and love that Christ would die for us. By whatever extent we imagine that we are lovable or worth His sacrifice we lessen our appreciation of His love. The Bible teaches that God loves us not because of who *we* are but because of who *He* is. "God is love" (1 John 4:16). If God loved us because something attractive or worthwhile within us elicited that love, then, changeable creatures that we are, we could lose that appeal and with it God's love. But if He loves us because God is love, then that love can never be lost, for God never changes. Therein lies our security for eternity (Jeremiah 31:3)—and all the glory is His!

We often find it difficult, especially in trying circumstances, to rest in God's great love for us—no doubt because deep within our hearts we know how unworthy we are. Christian psychology tries mistakenly to cure this sense of unworthiness by persuading us that we are worth it after all. One leading televangelist claims that Christ's death on the cross proves that "we really are somebodies!" No, Christ didn't die for *somebodies*, but for unworthy *sinners*. A Christian psychologist calls the cross "a foundation for self-esteem." Another adds, "If we hadn't been worth it He wouldn't have paid the price." On the contrary, the price was paid to *redeem us from sin*, not to establish our *worth*. That the sinless Son of God had to die upon the cross to redeem us shouldn't make us feel good about ourselves, but deeply ashamed, for it was our sins that nailed Him there.

This humanistic, self-inflating gospel is being increasingly embraced by evangelicals. Jay Adams points out the horrible error of teaching that what God does for us is "a response on His part to our significance rather than an act of His love, free mercy, goodness, and grace!"

Praise God that our song for eternity will be, "Worthy is the *Lamb*" (Revelation 5:12). Heaven has no place for the erroneous belief that Christ died because *we* are worth it. Christ's death in our place had nothing to do with our worth, but with the depths of our sin, the demands made by God's justice, and His eternal glory.

Of course those who brought humanistic psychology's selfism into the church attempt to support it from Scripture. One such person has quoted Psalm 139 and suggests that the "wonderful pattern for growth, fulfillment and development" that "God built into our genes...is the ultimate basis for self-esteem." Surely the genius of the genetic code should cause me to bow in wonder and worship at the wisdom and power of God—but *self*-esteem? Seeing the marvels of God's creative power in my genes is no more cause for *self*-exaltation than seeing God's creative power in another's genes or in any part of the cosmos—*I* didn't create it.

Paul declared, "By the grace of God I am what I am" (1 Corinthians 15:10). No basis for self-esteem there. Dare we think that we will ever be able to erase from our memories the fact that we are unworthy sinners saved by grace? Christ, as the lamb slain for sin, will forever bear the marks of Calvary. What significance would those marks have if we did not remember—not the depths and details of our sin— that we are redeemed by His blood from our sin?

Yes, God in His grace will give us crowns and rewards and we will even hear from our Lord's lips, "Well done, thou good and faithful servant...enter thou into the joy of thy [L]ord" (Matthew 25:21). But will that give us a positive self-image, a sense of self-worth and self-esteem? C.S. Lewis answers: "The child who is patted on the back for doing a lesson well...the saved soul to whom Christ says, 'Well done,' are pleased and ought to be. For here the pleasure lies not in what you are but in the fact that you have pleased someone you rightly wanted to please. The trouble begins when you pass from thinking, 'I have pleased him,' to thinking, 'What a fine person I must be to have done it.' "

Our love for God even influences whether we yield to temptation. Lust is called both "deceitful" (Ephesians 4:22) and "hurtful" (1 Timothy 6:9) because it entices us with pleasure that is brief and involves disobedience to God and thus leads to pain and ruin in the end. Those whose focus is upon themselves think of God's commandments in terms of pleasures denied. But those who are enraptured by God's love have been delivered from self and find true and lasting pleasure and joy in obeying and thus pleasing Him. There is a joy that comes from pleasing God that is so far beyond any pleasure of this world that temptation loses its power in comparison.

The new theology denies us this path of victory. Its joy is selfish. To obey the first and great commandment is necessarily to deny self as Christ commanded (Matthew 16:24). Nor can one deny self and at the same time love, esteem, and value self. Seeing God's love as a response to my significance and worth salvages just enough value for self to deny God's truth. Let us forget ourselves, our needs, and hurts, and seek to know and love God (Father, Son, and Holy Spirit) because of who He is and His love and grace to us. His love will then flow through us to others, whom we will then esteem better than ourselves (Philippians 2:3). Such is the path to true joy (Hebrews 12:2).

15

Knowing and Loving God

I count all things but loss for the excellency of the
knowledge of Christ Jesus my Lord: for whom I
have suffered the loss of all things…that I may
know him, and the power of his resurrection….
—PHILIPPIANS 3:8-10

During the temptation in the wilderness, Satan offered to give Jesus "all the kingdoms of the world…and the glory of them" (Luke 4:5,6). He was not bluffing. This world really is Satan's to give to whom he will. Jesus did not dispute Satan's boast that this world had been "delivered unto me [by God]; and to whomsoever I will I give it." The conditions upon which Satan offered this world to Christ were clear: "If you bow down and worship me"—which, of course, Jesus refused to do. Beware! For the kingdoms and glories of this world are still the favors Satan bestows in order to entice today's recipients into worshiping him.

Like their Lord, Christ's true followers refuse the kingdoms and glories of this world. This refusal includes the highly touted new world order, which will still be under

Satan's control. Christ has promised believers something far better—an eternal and heavenly kingdom procured through His defeat of Satan at the cross. As a result of that victory, "the kingdoms of this world [will] become the kingdoms of our Lord and of his Christ" (Revelation 11:15). Worldly kingdoms will soon pass away, and in their place the kingdom of God will come to earth. Then Christ, together with those who have shared in His rejection and suffering (Romans 8:17; 2 Timothy 2:12), will reign in glory and ultimate joy forever.

It would be a denial of their Lord for Christians to bask in the popularity and honors which this present world may bestow upon them. That is not to say that a Christian should never be successful in business, science, the academic world, sports, and so on. Indeed, Christians should be the very best they can possibly be at whatever they do. But their skill, talent, and diligent efforts are to be expended for God's glory, not for their own. This world has no attraction for believers; they neither love it nor its plaudits. They are not swayed from the course they must run (1 Corinthians 9:24-27; 2 Timothy 4:7,8) either by the world's criticism or its compliments. They know that ultimately nothing matters except God's opinion of them.

We are warned, "Love not the world, neither the things that are in the world. If any man love the world, the love of the Father is not in him" (1 John 2:15). Satan is called "the god of this world" (2 Corinthians 4:4), and those who love this world are siding with and honoring Satan, whether they realize it or not. Indeed, they are on the road to Satan worship, which will be the worldwide religion during the Great Tribulation (Revelation 13:4).

One evidence that Christianity has been seduced by Satan is the fact that those who are highly honored by the world are, on that basis alone, given instant and special honor in the church. The Christian media fawns over a sports hero, an attractive actress, a wealthy businessman, or a highly placed politician who has supposedly become a

Christian. These too-often immature, worldly new believers are paraded and lauded on Christian TV and held up to the church as heroes of the faith and role models for youth—and Christians turn out by the thousands to "ooh" and "aah" at their testimonies. Yet the humble, godly missionary, mature in the faith, who has remained true to Christ through decades of privation, temptation, hardship, and danger, and who has won souls in difficult fields of labor, can scarcely draw an audience.

Jesus told His disciples, "If ye were of the world, the world would love his own; but because ye are not of the world, but I have chosen you out of the world, therefore the world hateth you" (John 15:19). Thus, to Pilate, Jesus declared, "My kingdom is not of this world" (John 18:36). He did not mean that His kingdom is totally detached from this earth, but that it is not of this *world system*. In fact, it stands in opposition thereto. This present world system (including the new world order), which belongs to Satan, must be destroyed for the kingdom of God to be established.

Christ came to "destroy the works of the devil" (1 John 3:8), which He accomplished upon the cross (John 12:31-33). Such is His purpose in all those who receive Him as Savior and Lord. The works of Satan in and through our lives, and any attachment to this world, must be destroyed so that Christ can reign in us. This goal can only be effected through the work of His cross applied to one's daily life in the power of the Holy Spirit. Only to that extent will the love of God and His will and Christlike character be manifested in the hearts and lives of believers.

The unsaved love the world. In contrast, Christians do not love the world; they love the Father. We are citizens of heaven, "from whence also we look for the Saviour the Lord Jesus Christ: who shall change our vile body, that it may be fashioned like unto his glorious body, according to the working whereby he is able even to subdue all things unto himself" (Philippians 3:20,21). Instead of trying to make our mark in this world and to receive its benefits and enjoy its pleasures, we seek to please the Father because we desire a *heavenly* and *eternal* reward.

The choice we face is not, as many imagine, between heaven and hell. Rather, the choice is between heaven and this world. Even a fool would exchange hell for heaven; but only the wise will exchange this world for heaven. One cannot have both—"all this and heaven, too." One cannot live both for God and for self. Many who call themselves Christians find it difficult to resist the temptations of this world and to live wholly for Christ.

Why should it be difficult to choose life instead of death, joy instead of sorrow, eternal fulfillment instead of remorse, God's truth and love instead of Satan's lies and destructive lusts? The choice is only difficult for those who are deceived by Satan, and who thus, in believing this liar, doubt and dishonor God. What an insult it is to their heavenly Father for Christians to act as though surrendering to God's will were a great sacrifice—as though exchanging this world for heaven were a bad bargain.

Motivation is a key element. One powerful motivation comes through comparing the length of eternity with one's brief life on this earth. Only a fool would trade the heavenly and eternal for that which is earthly and temporal—and, remember, one cannot have both. "Christians" who habitually live for what they can accumulate and enjoy in this present world, instead of "lay[ing] up treasures in heaven" (Matthew 6:19-21) as Christ commanded, deny with their lives the faith they profess with their lips.

Those who repeatedly, in the daily choices they face, opt for this world instead of for heaven, should not be surprised when God gives them for eternity the choice they have made. How can one complain if he is not taken in the next life to the heaven he consistently rejected in this one? Someone has said there are only two kinds of people in the world: 1) those who say to God, "Not my will but Thine be done," and 2) those to whom God says, "Not My will, but thine, be done." What a tragedy to be chained for eternity to one's own will instead of His—forever imprisoned with self and separated from God.

Christ's declaration to the Father, "Not my will, but thine, be done" (Luke 22:42) put Him on the cross. Likewise, we must deny self in submission to the cross (Matthew 16:24). That submission puts an end to self, and Christ becomes our very life, our all. This is the path of wisdom (Job 28). The wise will "shine...as the stars for ever" (Daniel 12:3) with His light in their hearts—pure vessels eternally radiating His glory. Fools will experience the blackness of darkness forever and ever because they have insisted upon doing their own thing and being their fallen selves. Man's destiny is either eternal joy in the presence of God and His angels and saints or a lonely and eternal agony shut up to self.

William Law had the gift of expressing with unusual clarity the choice between heaven and this world. He pointed out that a man would be considered insane who spent his life planning the house, tennis court, swimming pool, and retirement condominium that he expected to build on Mars—yet someone who spent his life equally absorbed in planning, achieving, and enjoying such things in this world would be respected as successful and prudent. In fact, said Law, both men are fools. The first is obsessed with a world where he *cannot live*—while the other is attached to a world where he *cannot stay*. The degree of their folly differs only by a few short years.

What a tragedy to barter eternal life for the enjoyments of this brief world. The Bible does not say that sin has no pleasure; it says that the pleasures of sin can only be enjoyed "for a season" (Hebrews 11:25)—and a very short season at that, particularly when compared with the endless ages of eternity.

The phrase "eternal life" refers not only to the quantity of the life God offers, but to its quality—a quality of life

> Knowing God leads to holiness. He alone becomes one's consuming passion...

God wants us to begin to experience here and now. Jesus said that eternal life was *knowing* (not knowing *about*) God and His Son (John 17:3). Paul warned that Christ would one day take vengeance upon those who "know not God" (2 Thessalonians 1:8). In keeping with the truth of these and similar scriptures, evangelicals profess that they don't practice a religion *about* God but that they have a personal relationship with God. Unfortunately, this boast has become almost a cliché—one that sounds good in theory but for which there is often little practical evidence in daily life.

Recognizing that eternity is infinitely longer than one's most optimistic life expectancy provides a powerful motivation for living for Him (and thus choosing heaven instead of this world). But to truly know God provides an even more powerful motivation.

Knowing God leads to holiness. He alone becomes one's consuming passion, displacing all other desires and overcoming the power of sin in our lives. His presence within is sufficient to satisfy every longing. For to know God is to love Him—and there is no higher motivation for obedience to His commands than love. In fact, no other motivation is accepted. It is no accident that the first commandment is, "Thou shalt love the Lord thy God with all thine heart, and with all thy soul, and with all thy might" (Deuteronomy 6:5).

> Loving God is the secret of the Christian life. If we truly love Him, then we want to serve and please and glorify Him.

Obedience to God's laws must spring from love for Him. Otherwise, as 1 Corinthians 13:1-3 declares, obeying the letter of the law is nothing. We could give all our possessions to the poor and submit to martyrdom at the stake in service for Christ, but if our motive is not love it would all be in vain. So it is that Christ declared, "If a man love me he will keep my words...he that loveth me not keepeth not my sayings" (John 14:23,24).

Loving God is the secret of the Christian life. If we truly love Him, then we want to serve, please, and glorify Him. We would not want to do anything or even think a thought that would displease or dishonor Him. A genuine love for God—and only that love—produces consistent holiness in our daily lives. Love is also the great wellspring of joy and peace. It causes us to witness to the lost about us with passion and without shame. For who is ashamed of one's lover? And who does not rather speak well, boldly, and continually of the one he loves!

Where shall we find this love that we must have for God, and without which we cannot please Him? It is not hiding somewhere in our hearts waiting to be discovered. Nor is it a potential that we have which only needs to be developed. We cannot work it up. It cannot be produced by effort. This love is not in us at all. Though it involves our will and emotions, it comes from God alone.

How then is this love produced? Love is a fruit which the Spirit bears in our lives (Galatians 5:22). It is miraculous, like the fruit on a tree—something that only God could produce. Yet we are not like a tree, which has no will or emotions. Obviously much more is involved when the Spirit bears fruit in the believer's life than is involved in fruit-bearing in nature. His love is the key.

"We love him because he first loved us" (1 John 4:19) tells us that our love for God comes as a response to His love for us. We know of His love through His Word. Our hearts are stirred as we believe what the Bible tells us of God's love in creating us, giving His Son to die for our sins, patiently bearing our stubborn rejection, pardoning and saving us from the penalty that His holy law demands for our sin, providing heaven at infinite cost. Surely to meditate upon God's love for us must produce, by His Spirit, fervent love for Him.

Much more, however, is involved than reading and memorizing and believing what the Bible says *about* God and His love. Jesus reproved the Pharisees for searching the Scriptures and at the same time refusing to come to Him, the

One of whom the Scriptures testified. What the Bible says about God is there in order to lead us into a personal relationship with Him. We must know not only His Word, but we must know *Him* personally. There is an intimacy with God that is promised to those who love and thus obey Him, an intimacy which is missing in the lives of many Christians.

To those who love and obey Him, Christ offers an incredibly wonderful promise: "He that hath my commandments, and keepeth them, he it is that loveth me: and he that loveth me shall be loved of my Father, and I will love him, and will manifest myself to him" (John 14:21). This promise to manifest Himself to those who love Him implies a real communication of His presence. This is more than a strong belief that He is with us. It is a spiritual manifestation of His presence.

This intimate fellowship begins at conversion with a real communication from God's Spirit to the believer's spirit. God's spirit "beareth witness with our spirit that we are the children of God" (Romans 8:16). It is not simply putting one's name in John 3:16 and taking it "by faith." There is a *knowing* God, a very real *knowing* that we are His, and an ongoing communion with Him in prayer. This does not involve visualization, journaling, or any technique, but an intimacy that He initiates and promises to maintain with those who love and obey Him.

Most people, Christians included, would jump at the chance to become an intimate friend and confidant of a world leader, an astronaut, an Olympic gold medallist, the head of a multinational corporation, or a famous heart surgeon. How many, however, neglect the infinitely more wonderful opportunity to know the God who created the universe, to have continual and intimate fellowship with the One who has all power, all wisdom, all knowledge, and who loves us immeasurably! As with anyone else, God's companionship must be cultivated. It takes time. And we will only devote the time if we really believe that we can know God and that intimacy with Him is worthwhile.

"He is a rewarder of them that *diligently* seek [not success, pleasure, health, or wealth in this world, but] him"

(Hebrews 11:6). God said to Abram, "I [not land or cattle or other possessions that I will bless you with, but *I*] am thy shield and thine exceeding great reward" (Genesis 15:1). God wants to reward us with Himself. Let us not settle for any lesser rewards, for mere gifts instead of the Giver. Let us diligently pursue this intimate fellowship that He desires for each of us. Let us say with David, "O God...early will I seek thee: my soul thirsteth for thee" (Psalm 63:1); and with Paul, "That I may know him, and the power of his resurrection and the fellowship of his sufferings, being made conformable unto his death" (Philippians 3:10). And may knowing and loving God be our passion, as it was theirs.

16

The Problem of Self-Love

In the last days perilous times
shall come. For men shall be lovers
of their own selves....
—2 TIMOTHY 3:1,2

The apostle Paul warned that in the last days prior to Christ's return sound doctrine would be scorned and in its place professing Christians would turn to myths (2 Timothy 4:3,4). There appears to be a sad fulfillment of that warning in our day and as a result there is a diminishing biblical and increasing humanistic content in Christian books and sermons. The very foundations of the Christian faith are being undermined by many of those who are looked to as its chief defenders. Yet at the same time, most if not all of those involved in this destructive process stoutly and sincerely insist that what they teach is "biblical."

How is such delusion possible? It has been accomplished by a subtle redefinition. Whereas to be "biblical" used to mean that a teaching was *derived* from Scripture, it now means that it may be derived from anywhere so long as it can somehow be interpreted as being *compatible* with Scripture. Thus the Bible and Christ the Living Word are no longer "the truth" as Scripture so clearly claims. Instead, under the specious slogan that "all truth is God's truth," Holy Writ is now seen as only one of many ingredients in a new recipe for happiness to which anything may be added so long as the mixture still tastes somewhat "biblical." As a result, Christians are losing their taste and appetite for unadulterated truth.

This accelerating erosion of spiritual discernment is compounded by the fact that exegesis of Scripture has fallen into disfavor with both shepherds and sheep. Ears are being tickled instead with humanistic concepts which are introduced as allegedly necessary and helpful supplements to God's Word, complete and sufficient though it is in itself. Far from being helpful, however, these "supplements" subtly effect reinterpretations of Scripture—and a generation grows up with a "Christianity" whose foundations have been undermined without their knowing it.

Let's take a simple example. Jesus commanded His disciples, "But seek ye first the kingdom of God, and his righteousness; and all these things [food, clothing, shelter] shall be added unto you" (Matthew 6:33). From humanistic psychology, however (now a legitimate source of revelation according to the "all truth is God's truth" thesis), so-called Christian psychologists have borrowed another myth: Abraham Maslow's "hierarchy of needs." It states that man's physical needs for such things as food, clothing, and shelter must *first* be met, then so-called psychological needs, and *last of all* spiritual needs. Although it blatantly turns Christ's command upside down, Maslow's theory and its derivatives now permeate the books and sermons of many church leaders and influence evangelism. Biblical exegesis has been abandoned for a new source of "truth."

Let's take one more example. As we cited at the beginning of this chapter, Paul solemnly warns, "...in the last days perilous times shall come. For men shall be lovers of their own selves..." (2 Timothy 3:1,2). Then follows a list of sins which peculiarly characterize our world today and all of which have their root in self-love. Once again from humanistic psychology, however, Christian psychologists have borrowed the seductive myth that self-love (along with its concomitants self-esteem/worth/acceptance, and so on) is a vital ingredient for "mental health." Thus, instead of the prevalence of self-love, as the Bible declares, a lack of it is now stated to be the root of the sins listed in verses 2-4, which have been redefined as "behavior problems" requiring newly discovered "psychological solutions."

This pop psychology myth, having been introduced into Christianity by leaders of impeccable reputation, has become so popular that today it is the prevailing belief throughout the church. It is as though Paul actually wrote, "...in the last days perilous times shall come. For men shall be haters of their own selves, and as a consequence will need to undergo therapy and attend seminars in order to learn to love themselves properly...." Such mutilations would be required before one could derive the current self-love/self-worth fad from Scripture.

Acceptance of psychology's delusion that a lack of self-love is our major problem means that Christ's statement to "love your *neighbor* as yourself" has to be reinterpreted as a command to love *ourselves*. Why, if we all lack self-love, would Christ command us to love our neighbors as we [fail to] love ourselves? Christ's apparent error is now corrected by books and seminars teaching us how to first of all love self so that we can fulfill His command.

> We are thus commanded to manifest love for our neighbors in the same way; that is, by caring for them as we care for ourselves.

In contrast, simple exegesis of Christ's command to "love your neighbor as yourself" would *derive from Scripture* the following: 1) clearly we must already love ourselves, or such a command would be foolish; 2) this is confirmed by Ephesians 5:29 ("For no man ever yet hated his own flesh;

> "If ye continue in my word, then are ye my disciples indeed; and ye shall know the truth, and the truth shall make you free."
> —John 8:31,32

but nourisheth and cherisheth it..."), which is substantiated by the obvious fact that we feed, clothe, and care for ourselves and seek to satisfy our own desires; 3) we are thus commanded to manifest love for our neighbors in the same way; that is, by caring for them as we care for ourselves; and 4) the fact that this command is necessary indicates that, rather than lacking in self-love, our problem is an excessive amount of it, which causes us to be selfish and thus to neglect caring for others. It is this self-centeredness that Christ seeks to correct. Such had been the consistent interpretation of this Scripture for 1900 years until humanistic psychology was embraced as a valid source of "God's truth."

As a result, Christian leaders now promote the very love of self that Paul warned would characterize men in the last days and from which Christ came to deliver us by His cross.

That we must derive truth from the Bible itself and from no other source is clear from Christ's statement: "If ye continue in my word, then are ye my disciples indeed; and ye shall know the truth, and the truth shall make you free" (John 8:31,32). Simple exegesis indicates that the truth which alone sets us free from sin and self is: 1) revealed only through His Word, 2) understood only by those who "are of God" and obey ("if ye continue") His Word, and 3) hidden to all others (see verses 43-47). Each of these points is denied by the "all truth is God's truth" myth. It credits those "not of God" with revelations of "God's truth" which supplement the very Word of God which they steadfastly oppose.

Solomon wrote, "My son, give me thine heart, and let thine eyes observe my ways. For a whore is a deep ditch; and a strange woman is a narrow pit" (Proverbs 23:26,27). Here we have the simple ingredients of a godly life. There must first of all be the relationship to God as children ("My son...") born into His family by His Spirit. Then follows surrender of our hearts to Him ("give me thine heart"), which involves both love and commitment. Next we observe His ways, follow His example, obey His Word. How can we do this? Motivation comes through our love for Him and the wisdom imparted by His Word. No matter how pleasurable for the moment, unfaithfulness to God (as to one's spouse) and disobedience to His Word eventually become a deep ditch and a narrow pit bitter as death itself.

Why should husband and wife be faithful to one another? Why not so-called free sex? For one thing, sex is never "free," but always carries obligations and consequences that cannot be escaped. Of course it is possible for a husband or wife to "tire" of each other and to "fall in love" with someone else—but that is not real love. God's Word tells us that "love" is more than sexual passion or pleasure. The God-ordained relationship between male and female (like our relationship to Him) involves total commitment. The man who cheats on his wife or divorces her to marry a "more attractive" or "compatible" woman may enjoy what seems to be pleasure and fulfillment for a time. Eventually, however, the remorse for having broken his marriage vows and having dishonored the God who created him will turn illicit pleasure into great pain. Obedience to God's Word gives joy now and eternally. Exchanging that deep and lasting satisfaction for temporary pleasure is a bad bargain indeed.

Psychology, however, allows one to say, "I *can't* love my wife or husband or parent." Yet, as we have seen, we are *commanded* to love: first of all God, then our neighbor as ourselves, and finally even our enemies. True love comes from obedience to God's Word and is thus based upon commitment to sound doctrine. Nor is there any excuse under any circumstances for not loving spouse or parent, friend or foe, whether or not they mistreat or even hate us. The same is true of all of the ingredients of a happy, productive, fruitful, victorious life: they come from obedience to sound doctrine. Far from being divisive as some complain, doctrine is our very life. Those who will not endure it delude themselves with a false "Christianity" that will be severely judged for its fundamental disobedience.

The Bible does not say, "Rejoice in the Lord always... unless you are unable to do so because of an unhappy childhood, a bout of depression, or adverse circumstances." It does not say, "Be anxious for nothing...unless you have a nervous disposition." It does not say, "Forgive...unless you are unable to because of abuse." We are not excused from obeying the command, "Be not afraid" because we happen to be timid and fearful. Nor are we excused from the command, "Let the peace of God rule in your hearts" because we have been diagnosed as susceptible to stress. Nor are we excused from the command to love because we find certain people unlovable. Unfortunately, however, the simple obedience to God's Word that sound doctrine compels has been undermined by "psychological counseling" that nourishes unbelief and rebellion. Therapy then offers to justify our disobedience, to comfort us in our rebellion, and to provide the peace and joy that only God can give to those who trust and obey Him.

Love, joy, peace, longsuffering, gentleness, goodness, faith, meekness, and temperance (Galatians 5:22,23) are clearly declared to be the fruit not of therapy but of the Holy Spirit working in our lives. How? Through some magic process by which God "zaps" us and we are transformed? No, but as God's truth so grips our hearts that we are fully persuaded to be ruled by His Word, to obey Him, and to trust Him to fulfill in us what He has promised. This is not to deny the miraculous working of the Holy Spirit powerfully in our hearts and through us in others, in ways beyond human comprehension. It is merely to say that the Bible clearly declares that God works in our lives through our obedience to His Word. As Jesus said, "If ye continue in my word, then are ye my disciples indeed; and ye shall know the truth, and the truth shall make you free" (John 8:31,32).

The litmus test of truth for victorious Christian living must be: Is it *derived* from Scripture, or is it the wisdom of this world, packaged in Christian terminology in order to make it appear to be *compatible* with Scripture? This test should not only be applied to the sermons and writings of others, but to ourselves. We should each get on our knees and ask God, "How much of my daily life is rooted in Your Word, and how much is rooted in the world? When I am happiest, is it because I know I have pleased my heavenly Father, am rejoicing in His grace and love, and 'the joy of the LORD is my strength' (Nehemiah 8:10); or is it because I have achieved worldly goals that bring the same joy to those who 'know not God and obey not the gospel' (2 Thessalonians 1:8)?"

Jesus accused the Pharisees of establishing traditions that nullified Scripture. Even the clear command to "Honour thy father and mother" had been turned completely around by the Pharisees (Matthew 15:1-6). Christ indicted them with their having established a system of religion that allowed men seemingly to honor God outwardly while in their hearts they remained committed to self. What left men's hearts far from God while their lips seemed to praise Him? Christ summed up His indictment by declaring that Israel's religious leaders had substituted the traditions of men for the true doctrine of God's Word (verses 7-9).

The human traditions which Christ exposed and opposed had at least been developed by religious leaders who presumably were sincere in their desire to please God. The traditions of men, however, which Christian psychology has embraced and brought into the church have been developed by godless humanists and self-confessed atheists who openly oppose biblical Christianity. Indeed, their theories are a secular religion put forth in opposition to the gospel of our Lord Jesus Christ. Along with this same "leaven of the Pharisees," something even worse is fermenting in today's church. May God help us to boldly expose and oppose these deadly errors and to stand uncompromisingly for obedience to His Word.

17

The Importance of Understanding the Cross

I am crucified with Christ: nevertheless I live; yet not I, but Christ liveth in me.
—GALATIANS 2:20

Anti-Christian elements in the secular world would like very much to do away with all public display of the cross. Yet it is still seen atop tens of thousands of churches and in religious processions, often made of gold and even studded with preciousstones.

"For the preaching of the cross is to them that perish foolishness; but unto us which are saved it is the power of God."
—1 Corinthians 1:18

Most frequently, however, the cross is displayed as popular jewelry hanging around necks or dangling from ears. One wonders by what strange alchemy the bloodstained, rugged cross of torment upon which Christ suffered and died for our sins became so sanitized and glamorized.

No matter how it is displayed, even as jewelry or graffiti, the cross is universally recognized as the symbol of Christianity—and therein lies a serious problem. The cross itself rather than *what transpired upon it* 19 centuries ago has become the focus of attention, resulting in several grave errors. Its very shape, though devised by cruel pagans for punishing criminals, has become holy and mysteriously imbued with magic properties, fostering the delusion that displaying a cross somehow provides divine protection. Millions superstitiously keep a cross in their homes or on their person or make "the sign of the cross" to ward off evil and frighten demons away. Demons fear Christ, not a cross; and any who have not been crucified with Him display a cross in vain.

Paul declared, "For the preaching of the cross is to them that perish foolishness; but unto us which are saved it is the power of God" (1 Corinthians 1:18). So the power of the cross lies not in its display but in its preaching; and that preaching has nothing to do with the peculiar shape of the cross but with *Christ's death upon it* as declared in the gospel. The gospel is "the power of God unto salvation to every one that believeth" (Romans 1:16), not to those who wear or otherwise display or make the sign of the cross.

What is this gospel that saves? Paul states explicitly: "I declare unto you the gospel which I preached unto you...by which also ye are saved...how that Christ died for our sins according to the scriptures; and that he was buried, and that he rose again the third day according to the scriptures" (1 Corinthians 15:1-4). It comes as a shock to many that the gospel includes no mention of a cross. Why? Because a cross was not essential to our salvation. Christ had to be crucified to fulfill the prophecy concerning the manner of the Messiah's death (Psalm 22), not because the cross itself had anything to do with our redemption. What was essential was the shedding of Christ's blood in His death as foreshadowed in the Old Testament sacrifices, for "without shedding of blood is no remission [of sins]" (Hebrews 9:22); "for it is the blood that maketh an atonement for the soul" (Leviticus 17:11).

This is not to say that the cross itself has no meaning. That Christ was nailed to a cross reveals the horrifying depths of evil innate within every human heart. To be nailed naked to a cross and displayed publicly, to die slowly with taunts and jeers filling the air, was the most excruciatingly painful and humiliating death that could be devised. And that is exactly what puny man did to his Creator. We ought to fall on our faces in repentant horror, overcome with shame, for it was not only the screaming, bloodthirsty mob and derisive soldiers but our sins that nailed Him there!

> At the same time that the cross lays bare the evil in man, however, it also reveals the goodness, mercy, and love of God as nothing else could.

So the cross lays bare for all eternity the awful truth that beneath the polite façade of culture and education the heart of man is "deceitful above all things, and desperately wicked" (Jeremiah 17:9), capable of evil beyond comprehension even against the God who created and loves him and patiently provides for him. Does any man doubt the wickedness of his own heart? Let him look at the cross and recoil in revulsion from that self within. No wonder the proud humanist hates the cross.

At the same time, however, that the cross lays bare the evil in man, it also reveals the goodness, mercy, and love of God as nothing else could. In the face of such unspeakable evil, such diabolical hatred vented against Him, the Lord of glory, who could destroy this earth and all upon it with a word, allowed Himself to be mocked and falsely accused and scourged and nailed to that cross! Christ "humbled himself, and became obedient unto death, even the death of the cross" (Philippians 2:8). When man was doing his worst, God responded in love, not merely yielding Himself to His tormentors but bearing our sins and taking the judgment we justly deserved.

Here we encounter another serious problem: representations of the cross focus the emphasis upon the physical suffering of Christ as though that paid for our sins. On the contrary, that was what man did to Him and could only add to our condemnation. Our redemption came about through: His bruising by Jehovah and "his soul [being made] an offering for sin" (Isaiah 53:10); God laying "on him the iniquity of us all" (verse 6); and His bearing "our sins in his own body on the tree" (1 Peter 2:24).

The death of Christ is irrefutable evidence that God in righteousness must punish sin. The penalty must be paid, or there can be no forgiveness. That God's Son had to endure the cross even after crying to His Father in agonizing contemplation of bearing our sins, ("[I]f it be possible, let this cup pass from me" (Matthew 26:39)), is proof that there was no other way mankind could be redeemed. When Christ, the sinless, perfect Man and beloved of His Father, took our place, God's judgment fell upon Him in all its fury. What then must be the judgment of those who reject Christ and refuse the pardon offered in Him? We must warn them.

At the same time and in the same breath that we sound the alarm of coming judgment, we must also proclaim the good news that redemption has been provided and God's forgiveness is offered for the vilest of sinners. Nothing more evil could be conceived than crucifying God, yet it was from the cross that Christ in infinite love and mercy prayed, "Father, forgive them; for they know not what they do" (Luke 23:34). So the cross proves, too, that there is forgiveness for the worst of sins and sinners.

Tragically, however, the vast majority of mankind reject Christ. And here we face another danger—that in our sincere desire to see souls saved we adjust the message of the cross to avoid offending the world. Paul warned that care had to be taken not to preach the cross "with the wisdom of words, lest the cross of Christ should be made of none effect" (1 Corinthians 1:17). But surely the gospel can be explained in a new way that is more appealing to the ungodly than those old-time preachers presented it. Perhaps today's techniques for packaging and selling could be used to clothe the cross in music or a beat or entertaining presentation such as the world uses that would give the gospel a new relevancy or at least familiarity. Surely, psychology, too, can be drawn upon to provide a more positive approach. Let us not confront sinners with their sin and the gloom and doom of coming judgment, but explain that their behavior isn't really their fault so much as it is the result of abuse they have suffered. Are we not all victims? And didn't Christ come to rescue us from victimization and our low view of ourselves and to restore our self-esteem and self-confidence? Blend the cross with psychology and the world will beat a path to our churches, filling them with new members. Such is today's new evangelicalism.

Confronting such perversion, A.W. Tozer wrote: "If I see aright, the cross of popular evangelicalism is not the cross of the New Testament. It is rather a new bright ornament upon the bosom of a self-assured and carnal Christianity....The old cross slew men; the new cross entertains them. The old cross condemned; the new cross amuses. The old cross destroyed confidence in the flesh; the new cross encourages it...the flesh, smiling and confident, preaches and sings about the cross; before that cross it bows and toward that cross it points with carefully staged histrionics—but upon that cross it will not die, and the reproach of the cross it stubbornly refuses to bear."

Here is the crux of the issue. The gospel is designed to do to self what the cross did to those who hung upon it: put it utterly to death. This is the good news in which Paul exulted: "I am crucified with Christ!" The cross is not a fire escape from hell to heaven but a place where we die in Christ. Only then can we experience "the power of His resurrection" (Philippians 3:10), for only the dead can be resurrected. What joy that promise brings to those who long to escape the evil of their own hearts and lives; and what fanaticism it seems to those who want to cling to self and who therefore preach what Tozer called the "new cross."

Paul declared that in Christ the Christian is crucified to the world and the world to him (Galatians 6:14). That is strong language. This world hated and crucified the Lord whom we now love—and in that act it has crucified us as well. We have taken our stand with Christ. Let the world do to us what it did to Him if it will, but we will never again join in its selfish lusts and ambitions, its godless standards, its proud determination to build a utopia without God, and its neglect of eternity.

To believe in Christ is to admit that the death He endured for us is exactly what we deserve. Therefore, when Christ died we died in Him: "[W]e thus judge, that if one died for all, then were all dead [that is, all have died]: and that he died for all, that they which live should not henceforth live unto themselves, but unto him who died for them, and rose again" (2 Corinthians 5:14,15).

"But I'm not dead," is the earnest response. "Self is still very much alive." Paul, too, acknowledged, "For the good that I would I do not: but the evil which I would not, that I do" (Romans 7:19). Then what does "I am crucified with Christ" really mean in daily life? It doesn't mean that we are *automatically* "dead indeed unto sin, but alive unto God through Jesus Christ our Lord" (Romans 6:11). We still have a will and choices to make.

Then what power does the Christian have over sin that the Buddhist or good moralist doesn't have? First of all, we have peace with God "through the blood of his cross" (Colossians 1:20). The penalty has been paid in full, so we no longer try to live a good life out of fear that otherwise we will be damned, but out of love for the One who has saved us. "We love him, because he first loved us" (1 John 4:19); and love moves the lover to please the One loved at any cost. "If a man love me, he will keep my words" (John 14:23), our Lord said. The more we contemplate the cross and meditate upon the price our Lord paid for our redemption, the more we will love Him; and the more we love Him, the more we will desire to please Him.

Secondly, instead of struggling to overcome sin, we accept by faith that we died in Christ. Dead men can't be tempted. Our faith is not in our ability to act as

> "Ye are dead, and your life is hid with Christ in God."
> —Colossians 3:3

crucified persons but in the fact that Christ was crucified once and for all in full payment of the penalty for our sins.

Thirdly, after declaring that he was "crucified with Christ," Paul added, "nevertheless I live; yet not I, but Christ liveth in me: and the life I now live in the flesh I live by [faith in the Son of God], who loved me, and gave himself for me" (Galatians 2:20). The just "live by faith" (Romans 1:17; Galatians 3:11; Hebrews 10:38) in Christ; but the non-Christian can only put his faith in himself or in some self-help program or phony guru.

Tragically, many who call themselves Christians have not accepted the finality of the cross and the power of Christ's resurrection. They either do not understand or find it impossible to believe what the Scripture says: "Knowing that Christ being raised from the dead dieth no more; death hath no more dominion over him...reckon ye also yourselves to be dead indeed unto sin, but alive unto God through Jesus Christ our Lord" (Romans 6:9-12), "Nor yet that he [Christ] should offer himself often...but now once...hath he appeared to put away sin by the sacrifice of himself...Christ was once offered to bear the sins of many...we are sanctified through the offering of the body of Jesus once and for all...after he had offered one sacrifice for sins for ever, [He] sat down on the right hand of God...by one offering he hath perfected for ever them that are sanctified...there is [therefore] no more offering for sin" (Hebrews 9:25–10:18).

As Christ died, He cried in triumph, "It is finished," using a Greek expression found on ancient invoices indicating that they had been *paid in full*. There is a blessed finality to the cross that delivers us from insecurity. Christ need never, indeed can never, die for our sins again. It is equally impossible for those who have been "crucified with Christ" by faith in Him to be "uncrucified" and then crucified with Christ again. Paul declared, "For ye are dead, and your life is hid with Christ in God" (Colossians 3:3). What assurance for time and for eternity to those who believe this good news of the gospel!

18

The Cross
That Saves Us

For the preaching of the cross is to them that
perish foolishness; but unto us which are saved it
is the power of God.
—1 CORINTHIANS 1:18

In our great concern over the growing apostasy and in
our zeal to contend for the faith once for all delivered to the
saints, we must constantly take heed of our personal relationship with and testimony for our Lord. And to do this, we
must always keep foremost in our hearts and minds the
cross—not its shape, but what transpired upon it.

Scripture makes it very clear that the cross of Christ is the
heart of the message we preach, the determinant of our relationship to this evil world, and the secret of victory over the
world, the flesh, and the devil in our daily lives. Christ
reminded His listeners repeatedly that it was not possible to
be His disciple and thus a true Christian without denying
self and taking up the cross to follow Him. The Bible makes it
clear what this means, although there is also more depth of
truth in the cross than we will be able to fathom in this life.

Paul wrote, "I determined not to know any thing among you, save Jesus Christ and him crucified" (1 Corinthians 2:2). This characterized his consistent conduct and the message he preached. For him there was one important rule: "Not with wisdom of words, lest the cross of Christ be made of none effect" (1:17). We dare not compromise, dilute, or try to improve with man's wisdom the straightforward simplicity of the cross. To do so destroys its truth and power to save others and to deliver us from succumbing to daily trials and temptations.

We have a tendency to forget that "the preaching of the cross is to them that perish foolishness" (1:18). One of the greatest problems today is the often well-intentioned attempt to reinterpret the gospel to make it reasonable and acceptable to the natural or carnal man. Instead, the unchangeable message must change the thinking and lives of those who receive it or it cannot change their eternal destiny. Let that never be forgotten. That transforming power is missing, both from the gospel preached to the lost and from the Christian's life, when the sharp sword of the Word with its radical message of the cross has been sheathed in the popular psychologies and self-oriented thinking of our day.

What we are trying to say is illustrated through a man who had the most amazing testimony of anyone who ever lived. A resident of death row, he knew on the day of his execution, as footsteps came resolutely down the corridor, that he was going to die. When the door of his cell swung open, however, the jailer spoke these astonishing words: "You are being set free. Another man is dying in your place!"

> Nor would it have saved their souls had they died on crosses erected beside His. He had to die in their place.

Of course, I'm referring to Barabbas, the only man who ever lived who could *literally* testify, "Jesus died for me, in my place!" But Barabbas was not saved. Why? Simply because the death of Christ had freed him to live his own life.

Yet that is often today's self-centered understanding of the gospel: Jesus died for me so that I can live for myself, for worldly success and happiness, and go to heaven when I'm too old or too sick to enjoy earthly pleasures anymore. Against that false impression, A.W. Tozer wrote:

> Among the plastic saints of our times, Christ has to do all the dying and all we want is to hear another sermon about His dying—no cross for us, no dethronement, no dying. We remain king within the little kingdom of Mansoul and wear our tinsel crown with all the pride of a Caesar; but we doom ourselves to shadows and weakness and spiritual sterility.

People would come to Christ promising to follow Him wherever He would lead. His reply was simple: "Let Me make it very clear. I'm heading for a hill outside of Jerusalem called Calvary, where they will crucify Me. So if you intend to be true to Me to the end, take up your cross right now because that is where we're going."

Of course no one did that. Even His closest disciples all forsook Him and fled to save their own lives. Nor would it have saved their souls had they died on crosses erected beside His. He had to die in their place. But after His resurrection they were changed men, no longer afraid to die for their Lord. For then they understood and believed and gladly submitted to the truth: Christ had died in their place because they *deserved* to die. His death was not to deliver them from death, but to take them through death and out the other side into resurrection.

At last they understood and believed. Acknowledging that God was just in condemning them to death for their rebellion against Him, they accepted the death of Christ their Savior as their very own. They had died in Him; and believing that changed everything.

In Galatians 6:14 Paul writes, "But God forbid that I should glory, save in the cross of our Lord Jesus Christ, by whom the world is crucified unto me, and I unto the world." As those who have been crucified with Christ, we have been completely cut off from this world. One of the problems with today's Christianity is its attempt to make itself appealing to the spirit of this world and thus to become popular with the world. Christ would no more be popular today than He was in His day; and He said that those who hated Him would hate His disciples. So John wrote, "Love not the world,

> "That through death he might destroy him that had the power of death, that is the devil; and deliver them who through fear of death were all their lifetime subject to bondage."
> —Hebrews 2:14,15

neither the things that are in the world. If any man love the world, the love of the Father is not in him" (1 John 2:15).

Inspired by the Holy Spirit, Paul explained further: "For though he was crucified through weakness, yet he liveth by the power of God. For we also are weak in him, but we shall live with him by the power of God toward you" (2 Corinthians 13:4). How are we weak in Him? Not in our relationship to sin or Satan or to the temptations of this world, over which we have the victory through Christ. We are weak in the same way that He was weak, that is, in that He did not fight to defend Himself or His kingdom against the political or military might of this world. His victory (and ours in Him) over Satan also came in submitting to death: "That through death he might destroy him that had the power of death, that is the devil; and deliver them who through fear of death were all their lifetime subject to bondage" (Hebrews 2:14,15).

It is not through gritting our teeth and determining by our willpower that we overcome temptation, but in accepting the fact that we are dead in Christ. The dead no longer lust, lose their tempers, or act selfishly. Our victory is in being "dead indeed unto sin, but alive unto God through Jesus Christ our Lord" (Romans 6:11). We have given up life as we would live it in order to experience His life being lived in and through us. The life He gives is resurrection life, and only those who are dead can receive that. We cannot know the fullness of the power of the Holy Spirit, which is the Spirit of Christ, until we have willingly accepted His death as our death.

These few thoughts scarcely scratch the surface of the meaning of the cross (which includes, of course, the resurrection). In meditating upon this greatest event of all time and eternity, we begin to see both the horror of our sin and the amazing love of our Lord—the two chief motivations for holiness. May we abide in His love, that the cross so fully proved, and become the messengers and channels of that love to the world for which He died.

19

Victory over Sin

But thanks be to God, which giveth us the victory through our Lord Jesus Christ.
—2 CORINTHIANS 15:57

Torn between their sincere desire to serve and honor their Lord and the inner turmoil of fleshly lusts and the seductive pull of worldly pleasures and honors, many Christians struggle to live for Christ. For them, Christianity involves great effort, little joy, much frustration and disillusionment, and the loss (when they have enough willpower to deny themselves) of so much they once enjoyed in life. They struggle to avoid Paul's list of "don'ts" in Colossians 3:5-8: "Mortify therefore your members which are upon the earth; fornication, uncleanness, inordinate affection, evil concupiscence, and covetousness, which is idolatry...put off all these; anger, wrath, malice, blasphemy, filthy communication out of your mouth." Failing repeatedly, they repent remorsefully and puzzle over their inability to live as they know they should—but seemingly can't.

They fare no better with Paul's list of "do's" that follows (verses 12-17); "Put on therefore, as the elect of God, holy and beloved, bowels of mercies, kindness, humbleness of mind, meekness, longsuffering; forbearing one another, and forgiving...put on charity....Let the word of Christ dwell in you richly....and whatsoever ye do in word or deed, do all in the name of the Lord Jesus, giving thanks to God and the Father by him."

Is it really possible to be sweet, kind, humble, loving, and forgiving at all times? The spirit is willing, but the flesh proves ever to be embarrassingly weak. How can one live up to the high standards the Bible sets for Christian living? Is there some secret to victory we are overlooking?

The two key expressions, "mortify" in verse 5 and "put on" in verse 12, only increase the bewilderment and sense of failure. Is it really possible to "put to death" ungodly desires and, shedding that body of evil, as it were, to be clothed in a resurrection body of godliness? Surely Paul, led of the Holy Spirit, is not taunting us with goals that cannot be attained and that, in fact, are not at all practical. Was he not himself an example of this kind of life, and did he not say more than once, "Be ye followers of me even as I also am of Christ" (1 Corinthians 4:16; 11:1)? Then why do we fail? From whence comes the motivation and the strength to accomplish what is at once so desirable and yet so seemingly impossible?

There is a general failure to recognize the importance of one little word that occurs in both verses 5 and 12. It holds the answer to our dilemma. Paul does not say, "Mortify your members" and "Put on bowels of mercies, kindness..." That would impose a "do-it-yourself" religion of gritting one's teeth in determination and struggling to live up to high moral standards—no different from the atheist's or Buddhist's attempt to do the same. That is not Christianity. Paul carefully and pointedly says, "Mortify *therefore*...Put on *therefore*..." Clearly *therefore* refers to something that Paul is convinced gives the Christian the motivation and power to do what he is commanding and lifts the Christian above the impossible struggle of flesh trying to live a godly life. It is, *therefore*, the Christian's secret to a happy, fruitful, and holy life that is pleasing to God.

The mortifying of the old deeds and the putting on of the new is possible only because, as the previous verses declare, "Ye are dead, and your life is hid with Christ in God" (Colossians 3:3). Certainly the same thing could not be said of the followers of Buddha, Muhammad, Krishna, and others. Christianity is thus unique and separated from all religions. Herein lies the secret dynamic of the Christian life. Why, then, doesn't every Christian experience this power in daily living? Sadly, many who call themselves Christians have a very superficial understanding of the gospel they claim to have embraced. "[H]ow that Christ died for our sins according to the scriptures; and that he was buried, and that he rose again the third day..." (1 Corinthians 15:3,4).

For many who believe that Christ died for their sins, this event is more mystical than historical. The horrible death of the cross is something that happened to Christ but which has only a theoretical rather than practical connection to them. Some may have such a faulty understanding of what Christ's death means that they are not true Christians at all. They have imagined that the death of Christ in their place delivered them from their deserved eternal punishment in hell, so that, like Barabbas, they could live as they pleased. They have never desired what Paul rejoiced in: "I am crucified with Christ: nevertheless I live; yet not I, but Christ liveth in me: and the life which I now live in the flesh I live by the faith of the Son of God, who loved me, and gave himself for me" (Galatians 2:20).

Paul was not expressing an inspiring but empty platitude. For that great apostle, the cross was no mere religious symbol, but the place where he had died to life as he would have lived it and had begun to experience the very life of Christ being lived in him. He knew that Christ gives resurrection life; *therefore* only those who have died in Christ can experience it. With wonder, amazement, and deep gratitude he realized that Christ had actually taken his place before a righteous, holy God—and that God had put Christ to death in payment for his (Paul's) sins. *Therefore*, Paul was a dead man. Christ's death in his place was literally his own death, and he rejoiced in that fact. If he was to experience life thereafter, it must be the resurrected Christ living in him. This is not mysticism, but is to be our daily experience *by faith*.

The transformation in Paul was at once remarkable, yet not surprising. The most seductive temptation Satan can devise will arouse no response from a dead man. Insult a dead man to his face and he will not retaliate in anger. As a dead man, Paul experienced a new freedom over sin that he had never known before. Yet, in spite of being dead, Paul was more alive than he had ever been: "I am crucified...nevertheless, I live." Dead to sin, he was alive to God through Christ. So real was this to Paul that it was as though Christ Himself were living in him—and, indeed, He was! Christ had become his very life—and this, said Paul, was what Christianity was all about.

Paul reminded the saints at Colossae that victory over sin and self was not possible through willpower and fleshly struggle. True victory could only come through understanding and believing what Christ's death for their sins and resurrection for their justification really meant. Paul declared that this was the secret of his own complete transformation—and so it must be with them.

But how could Christ's death, burial, and resurrection be as real to them as it was to Paul—so real that their very lives would be totally transformed? Paul explained: They must believe that Christ was coming any moment to take them to heaven, where they would thereafter appear with Him in glory. It was the hope of Christ's imminent return that would make the difference between victory and defeat in the Christian life!

That this hope is the key to victorious living is clear. Notice again Paul's staggering declaration: "When Christ, who is our life, shall appear, then shall ye also appear with him in glory. Mortify *therefore*...." That was such a vibrant hope and of such certain fulfillment that Paul began this entire section with the statement, "If ye then be risen with Christ, seek those things which are above, where Christ sitteth on the right hand of God. Set your affection on things above, not on things on the earth" (verses 1,2). Herein lies the secret to the godly life that Paul himself

> By His cross we have been cut off from this world just as surely as He has been.

lived and expected of the Colossians as well. They were to be so heavenly minded that the things of this earth would have no appeal and thus no power over them.

Nor was this orientation away from earth toward heaven to be merely a "mental attitude" they had adopted without any basis in reality. It was not wishful "positive thinking," but truth that would change their lives. Through Christ's cross Christians have been crucified to the world and the world has been crucified to them, as Paul so firmly declared (Galatians 6:14). A man who has just been taken down, dead, from a cross has no interest in this world nor does it have any claims upon him. The person crucified and those who crucified him have nothing further to do with each other. So it is with the Christian and the world through the cross of Christ. The vicious hatred this world has for Christ, and its irreconcilable animosity against all that He stands for, have been fully exposed in its rejection and crucifixion of our Lord. Christ declared that the world would hate and persecute us as it had Him (John 15:18-20; 16:2; 17:14). By His cross we have been cut off from this world just as surely as He has been.

Death, however, did not end it all. Christ rose triumphant from the grave and ascended to the right hand of the Father in heaven. Moreover, He is coming again in power and glory to judge and take vengeance upon those who have rejected Him—and we, who have identified ourselves with Him in His rejection and death, will participate in His triumph and glory. Nor is that Second Coming so far in the future that it has no practical meaning for us now. On the contrary, the rapture (which precedes the Second Coming) could occur today. The glorious fulfillment of the hope that the gospel has instilled within our hearts could burst upon us at any moment! This fact causes eternity to invade the present and makes the Christian no longer of this world.

Hear Paul say it again: "For ye are dead, and your life is hid with Christ in God." Consenting to be dead and willing for Christ to be their life was not only the Colossians' basis for victory, but the essential meaning of the gospel they must embrace. Otherwise, there could be no salvation. Without that they were mere Barabbases, grateful that Christ had died in their place, but mistakenly assuming that they had been "saved" in order to live for self. If they were not willing to acknowledge Christ's death as their very own and to give up life as they would have lived it so that Christ could become their life, then they could not experience the victory over sin and self that Paul preached. Indeed, they had not consented to the message of the gospel at all.

And what made the fact of their death, burial, and resurrection with Christ the dynamic power that transformed their lives? It was this promise: "When Christ, who is our life, shall appear, then shall ye also appear with him in glory." Once that truth had gripped their hearts so that His "appearing" to His own to take them to His Father's house in heaven had become their daily expectation and hope, Christ's death and resurrection were so real to them in the present that they were changed into new persons. As such, Paul told them, they were to "seek those things which are above, where Christ sitteth on the right hand of God. Set your affection on things above, not on things on the earth" (verses 1,2). May we each pursue that challenge wholeheartedly.

The "pretribulation rapture" is thus no mere hair-splitting thesis for theologians to discuss or a theory without practical effect. It is the overlooked secret to victory in the Christian's life. John said, "Every man that hath this hope in him purifieth himself, even as he [Christ] is pure" (1 John 3:3). Paul indicated that it had been his love of Christ's appearing that had motivated him to holiness and faithfulness and had made him victorious—and that the same "crown of righteousness" was for "all them also that love his [Christ's] appearing" (2 Timothy 4:8). On the other hand, Christ associated wickedness with failing to love His appearing (Matthew 24:48-51).

Let us diligently and enthusiastically "seek those things that are above, where Christ sitteth on the right hand of God." Let us "set [our] affection on things above, not on things on the earth." Why? "For our conversation [citizenship] is in heaven; from whence also we look for the Saviour, the Lord Jesus Christ: who shall change our vile body, that it may be fashioned like unto his glorious body, according to the working whereby he is able even to subdue all things unto himself" (Philippians 3:20,21). Praise God!

20

"In Everything Give Thanks"

Enter into his gates with thanksgiving,
and into his courts with praise:
be thankful unto him, and bless his name.
—Psalm 100:4

For many Americans, the word "thanksgiving" means little more than a holiday from work or school, an excuse to overeat and watch special sports events. The fourth Thursday of every November is hardly devoted to giving of thanks. And what brief thanks is given to God scarcely reflects habitual attitudes. How readily we return to lives devoted to self instead of to Him—lives characterized more by complaining than by gratitude.

This chapter is not intended as an exhortation to sanctify a secular holiday. Rather, we want to deal with something much deeper, something which ought to characterize our lives at all times. Sadly, that continual thanksgiving which Scripture exhorts—"giving thanks *always*" (Ephesians 5:20)—is a rare commodity among Christians. Why? And how can our attitudes be changed?

Christian psychologists and motivational speakers would suggest that "exchanging grumbling for gratitude turns unhappiness into joy." Now there's a catchy phrase to motivate thanksgiving, or so it would seem. Those who are deceived by such slogans adopt a thankful "mental attitude" for selfish reasons—in order to benefit themselves. Such placebo techniques may produce surface changes and even convince those who seem to benefit for a time, but eventually the forced smiles betray empty hearts.

It is God's truth, and only God's unique truth, which can effect any real and lasting transformation in our lives. Furthermore, there is always much for which we ought to be genuinely and continuously thankful. Most people who think they have nothing to be thankful for are not nearly as bad off as they could be, and are far better off than millions of others—reason enough to be thankful. No matter how dismal one's circumstances may seem, there is always a great deal for which to give thanks. But the problem goes deeper.

It is self on the throne, wanting to please and benefit itself—and the failure to deny self as Christ commanded—which brings unhappiness no matter how favorable circumstances may be. Fear of loss haunts those whose security and joy is in earthly position and possessions; and death eventually robs them of all. Genuine and acceptable thanksgiving to God must have a source far deeper than a feeling of gratitude for the physical blessings of this temporary and fragile earthly existence.

> Our hearts should be continually filled to overflowing with thanksgiving to the God who created and redeemed us.

The trials of this brief life will soon be ended—either through death or the rapture. The Christian knows that though this body of flesh and blood may die and decay, he has a new body "eternal in the heavens" (2 Corinthians 5:1) which will never know pain, fatigue, or death. We have "an inheritance incorruptible, and undefiled, and that fadeth not away, reserved in heaven for [us], who are kept by the power of God through faith unto salvation..." (1 Peter 1:4,5). Here is truth that ought to grip our hearts and make us always thankful—truth so wonderful that one would think we could never thank God enough. When did you last thank Him for eternal life?

As Christians our hearts should be continually filled to overflowing with thanksgiving to the God who created and redeemed us. How wonderful that though we

> Thanksgiving, however, is not enough. It should always lead to praise.

sinned so grievously against Him and were His enemies, He became a man to suffer for our sins. His Holy Spirit pursued and wooed us to Himself with infinite love even when we persisted in our self-centered rebellion. What grace! What love! How can we take these blessings for granted?

The very life we have, with the capacity to know and love one another and, wonder of wonders, to know and love God and enjoy His love, is a priceless gift. What gratitude should flood our hearts and lives and what fervent thanksgiving we ought to express to Him continually! And on top of it all, He has given us the surpassing privilege and joy of experiencing Christ's life within our mortal flesh and witnessing for Him in deed and word right now. What thanks ought to burst forth continually from our hearts to Him!

Thanksgiving, however, is not enough. It should always lead to praise. And there is a difference. Thanks expresses appreciation for what God has done to benefit the one who is thankful. Praise goes beyond thanksgiving. It highly values, exalts, commends, extols, glorifies, and honors God for whatever He has done and especially for who He is. Praise takes us from the mundane to the majestic, out of ourselves into Him. It values God above all else. Thus, praise can only flow from a heart that has come to *know* God.

How can we fully know God? Must not the praise of finite beings always reflect an imperfect understanding of Him who is infinite? Is it not an insult to evaluate God as less than He is? Then how can anyone truly praise Him? Yet Scripture says we can and must. Though praise is conceived in our imperfect perception of God, it matures into wonder and worship. Praise is made acceptable when it is amplified by the sense of awe that God is infinitely beyond our comprehension. That humble realization draws us closer to Him, sinks us deeper into His love, and compels us to seek to know Him better.

The passion of David's heart, like Paul's, was to know God and to be continually enjoying His presence: "My soul thirsteth for God" (Psalm 42:2; 63:1); "One thing have I desired of the LORD, that will I seek after; that I may...behold the beauty of the LORD" (Psalm 27:4); "I count all things but loss for the excellency of the knowledge of Christ Jesus my Lord...that I may know him" (Philippians 3:8-10). Could anything else be more worthwhile? "Turn your eyes upon Jesus; Look full in His wonderful face; And the things of earth will grow strangely dim In the light of His glory and grace."

As a young Christian I thought that Hebrews 11:6 ("he that cometh to God must believe that he is, and that he is a rewarder of them that diligently seek him") was the formula for getting things from God. If I would seek Him, as the verse prescribed, then He would reward me with the "things of earth" that I wanted. How could I have missed the fact that I was to "diligently seek *Him*"? And how could I truly seek Him if what I really wanted was not Him at all but other things? And would it not be a bad bargain indeed if, instead of God as my reward, I received things?

What can the result be when all we want is God and He rewards us with Himself? It can't be less than a taste of heaven here on earth. "Joy unspeakable and full of glory" (1 Peter 1:8). Heaven? We give it too little thought. It's the place where everyone wants to go—but not just yet. For many Christians heaven is a last resort, welcome only when they are too old or too ill to enjoy any longer the deceitful pleasures of this evil world.

How can we truly desire God's presence in our lives here and now if we would only reluctantly exchange earth for heaven? To be in heaven is to be in His presence. Do we really desire and enjoy God's presence? Wouldn't that be like being in church all the time—bored, restless, watching the clock, eager for it to end? What an indictment! And what further proof is needed that there is very little of God in most churches in spite of claims to the contrary.

God is a God of joy. To be in His presence is to be supremely happy. Jesus welcomes to heaven His faithful followers with these words: "Enter thou into the joy of thy Lord" (Matthew 25:21,23). Joy eternal? David knew it: "in thy presence is fullness of joy; at thy right hand there are pleasures for evermore" (Psalm 16:11). We begin to know that joy even now in this life as we give ourselves totally into His hands and rest in His love, trusting Him completely. That is when we begin to experience with wonder, "The joy of the Lord is your strength" (Nehemiah 8:10).

A favorite hymn begins, "There's joy in following Jesus, every moment of every day." Great joy for us and for Him: "He will rejoice over thee with joy...he will joy over thee with singing" (Zephaniah 3:17). Even the prophets who pronounced doom upon the disobedient knew this joy in their own hearts and lives: "I will joy in the God of my salvation" (Habakkuk 3:18). The closer to God we walk in holiness, the greater our joy: "and let thy saints shout for joy" (Psalm 132:9). As the hymn writer put it, "When God is near my heart is filled with ecstasy, And all the world's a paradise when God is near."

Then "let us draw near with a true heart in full assurance of faith" (Hebrews 10:22). He has opened the way for this intimate fellowship with the shedding of His blood for our sins—but our hearts must respond. As the bumper sticker used to say, "If God seems far away, guess who moved?"

Though the circumstances of this brief life on earth may have worsened, God has not changed. Our earthly condition, no matter how difficult, is temporary and will soon be past— but our heavenly home is eternal and remains secure. That hope brings present joy: "Now the God of hope fill you with all joy and peace *in believing*" (Romans 15:13). Yes, in *"believing*, ye rejoice with joy unspeakable and full of glory" (1 Peter 1:8)—a joy that makes us strong enough to live above our circumstances and to demonstrate to all who observe us that God is good and that we are in His hands.

There is much talk about "spiritual warfare" these days, and it often involves much error and extremism. So many Christians spend time "rebuking" demons, time that would be much better spent in praising God. Instead of focusing so much attention upon Satan and giving him so much credit, let us give thanks that "greater is he that is in [us] than he that is in the world" (1 John 4:4). Here is victory: in thanksgiving, praise, and joy!

Part IV

Deepening Our Faith

21

Understanding the Trinity

*In him dwelleth all the fulness of the Godhead
bodily.*
—COLOSSIANS 2:9

It is popularly taught (in Alcoholics Anonymous, for example, and by many religious leaders) that whatever idea one has of "God" is acceptable. Even Mother Teresa said, "Whatever God is in your mind you must accept." Jesus however, repudiated that idea. He said, "And this is life eternal, that they might know thee the only true God, and Jesus Christ, whom thou hast sent" (John 17:3). In fact, all through the Bible we are told that we must know and honor the true God alone and are warned against false gods. The first commandment is: "I am the Lord thy God...thou shalt have no other gods...thou shalt not bow down thyself to them, nor serve them" (Exodus 20:2-5).

Of course, in order to know the true God and to be kept from following false gods, we must have a clear understanding of who God is. Many people think of God as some "higher power" or mysterious "cosmic energy source" or

Mother Earth or the universe itself; and they convince themselves that it really doesn't matter how one perceives of "God" so long as one has some concept of Deity. False concepts of God, however, are an insult to the Creator God and they become the front for demons: "The things which the Gentiles sacrifice [to idols], they sacrifice to devils, and not to God" (1 Corinthians 10:20). Holding and honoring false concepts of "God" constitute a rejection of God and will consign those who cling to them to eternal separation from His presence.

The one true God calls us to understand and know Him: "And ye shall seek me, and find me, when ye shall search for me with all your heart" (Jeremiah 29:13). He does not reveal Himself to those who seek false gods. He only reveals Himself to those who seek to know Him as He truly is. And that knowledge comes through understanding: "But let him that glorieth glory in this, that he understandeth and knoweth me..." (Jeremiah 9:24), "...the Son of God is come, and hath given us an understanding, that we may know him that is true, and...his Son Jesus Christ. This is the true God, and eternal life...keep yourselves from idols" (John 5:20,21).

And that brings us to the controversial concept of the Trinity which is held uniquely by Christians. Critics argue that the word "Trinity" is not even found in the Bible. While that is true, the teaching is clear all through Scripture, in both the Old and New Testaments, that the biblical God is three persons, Father, Son, and Holy Spirit, who are yet One.

To deal with that issue, we must begin with God, as the Bible itself does: "In the beginning God created the heaven and the earth" (Genesis 1:1). The question immediately rises, "Who is this Creator God?" The creation He made reveals His eternal existence without beginning, His infinite power and infinite wisdom, but it cannot reveal His character and justice and His loving plan for man. These are fully revealed exclusively in the Bible.

As far as human religion and philosophy are concerned, there are two general concepts of God: 1) pantheism/

naturalism, that the universe itself is God; and 2) supernaturalism, that the Creator is distinct from His creation. Within these are two further views which oppose one another: 1) polytheism, that there are many gods; and 2) monotheism, that there is only one true God as the Bible declares.

Monotheism itself is divided into two further rival beliefs: 1) that God is a single being, and 2) that God has always existed in three persons who are separate and distinct yet One. While the Jewish Scriptures of the Old Testament clearly teach the Trinity, Judaism of today rejects it. This leaves Christians as the only ones who hold to that view. In fact, even some who call themselves Christians reject the Trinity. Yet it is the only logically and philosophically coherent view of God possible. Above all, this is what the Bible teaches.

Pantheism has the same fatal flaws as atheism. If everything is God, to be God has lost all meaning and so nothing is God. The problems with polytheism are equally obvious. There is no real God who is in charge, so the many gods fight wars and steal one another's wives. There's no basis for morals, truth, or peace in heaven or earth. Polytheism's basic problem is *diversity without unity*.

> God is complete in Himself, being three Persons: Father, Son, and Holy Spirit, separate and distinct, yet at the same time eternally one God.

The belief that God is a single being is held by both Muslims and Jews, who insist, respectively, that Allah and Jehovah are single entities. This belief is also held by pseudo-Christian cults such as Jehovah's Witnesses and Mormons—and by various aberrant Christian groups who also deny the deity of Christ. Some Pentecostals claim that God is a single being and that Father, Son, and Holy Spirit are God's three "titles" or "offices." Here we have *unity without diversity*.

That God must have both unity and diversity is clear. The god who is a single entity (Allah of Islam or the Jehovah of

Jehovah's Witnesses and Judaism, for instance), is incomplete in himself, unable to experience love, fellowship, and communion before creating beings with whom he could have these experiences. The Bible says that "God *is* love." But the god of Islam and Judaism could not be love in and of itself—for whom could it love when it was alone before creation?

The belief that God is a single entity (Unitarianism) and not three Persons existing eternally in one God (Trinitarianism) was first formulated in the early church around A.D. 220 by a Libyan theologian named Sabellius. He attempted to retain biblical language concerning Father, Son, and Holy Spirit without acknowledging the triune nature of God. Sabellius claimed that God existed as a single Being who manifested Himself in three activities, modes, or aspects; as Father in the creation, as Son in redemption, and as Holy Spirit in prophecy and sanctification. This ancient heresy, though condemned by the vast majority of Christians, survives to this day among many who call themselves Christians.

The Bible presents a God who did not need to create any beings to experience love, communion, and fellowship. This God is complete in Himself, being three Persons: Father, Son, and Holy Spirit, separate and distinct, yet at the same time eternally one God. They loved and communed and fellowshipped with each other and took counsel together before the universe, angels, or man were brought into existence. Isaiah "heard the voice of the Lord [in eternity past] saying, Whom shall *I* send, and who will go for *us*?" (Isaiah 6:8). Moses revealed the same counseling together of the Godhead: "And God said, Let *us* make man in *our* image, after *our* likeness"; and again, "Let *us* go down, and there confound their language" (Genesis 1:26; 11:7). Who is this "us" if God is a single entity? Why does God say, "The man is become as one of *us*" (Genesis 3:22)?

Moreover, if God is a single Being, then why is the plural Hebrew noun *elohim* (literally "gods") used for God repeatedly? In fact, this plural noun is in the center of Israel's famous confession of the *oneness* of God. The *Shema* declares, "Hear, O Israel, The LORD our God is one LORD" (Deuteronomy 6:4; Mark 12:29). In the Hebrew it reads, "Jehovah our *elohim* [gods] is one [*echad*] Jehovah." The Hebrew word *echad* allows for a unity of more than one. For example, it is used in Genesis 2:24 where man and woman become *one* flesh, in Exodus 36:13 when the various parts "became *one* tabernacle," and in 2 Samuel 2:25 when many soldiers "become *one* troop."

Nor is the word *elohim* the only way in which God's plurality is presented. For example: Psalm 149:2, "Let Israel rejoice in him that made him" (literally "makers"); Ecclesiastes 12:1, "Remember now thy Creator (literally "creators"); and Isaiah 54:5, "For thy Maker is thine husband (literally "makers, husbands"). Unitarianism has no explanation for this consistent presentation of God's plurality all through the Old Testament. Although the word "Trinity" does not occur in the Bible, the concept is clearly there, providing the unity and diversity which makes possible the love, fellowship, and communion within the Godhead. Truly the Trinitarian God is love—and He alone.

Jesus said, "The Father loveth the Son and hath given all things into his hand" (John 3:35). God's love is not just toward mankind but first of all among the three Persons of the Godhead. And three Persons they must be. Father, Son, and Holy Spirit can't be mere offices, titles, or modes in which God manifests Himself, for such cannot love, consult, and fellowship together. Not only is the Son presented as a Person, but so are the Father and the Holy Spirit. The Bible presents each as having His own personality: each wills, acts, loves, cares, can be grieved or become angry. "Offices" or "titles" don't do that. Unitarianism isn't biblical—and it robs the Godhead of the necessary qualities of true Deity.

> As Father, Son, and Holy Spirit are one God, so when the Son became man He brought that fullness of the Godhead with Him into flesh.

Godhead? Is that a biblical term? Yes, indeed. It occurs three times in the King James New Testament in Acts 17:29, Romans 1:20, and Colossians 2:9. In contrast to *theos*, which is used consistently throughout the New Testament for "God," three different but related Greek words occur in these verses (*theios, theiotes, theotes*), which the King James translators carefully designated by the special word, *Godhead*. That very term indicates a plurality of being. Paul wrote, "In him dwelleth all the fulness of the Godhead bodily" (Colossians 2:9). Did he simply mean that in Christ dwelt all the fullness of Himself? That would be like saying that in me dwells all the fullness of me. Does he simply mean that in Christ dwells all the fullness of Deity (as non-KJV translations render it)? That, too, would be redundant—or it would detract from the Deity of Christ. For if Christ is intrinsically God, then what is the point of saying that "in Him dwells all the fulness of Deity"? But if Christ is the Son and there are two other persons in the Godhead, then it does mean something. It means that just as Father, Son, and Holy Spirit are one God, so when the Son became man He brought that fullness of the Godhead with Him into flesh.

In Romans 1:20 Paul argues that God's "eternal power and Godhead" are seen in the creation He made. God's eternal power—but His Godhead? Yes, as Dr. Wood pointed out years ago in *The Secret of the Universe*, the triune nature of God is stamped on His creation. The cosmos is divided into three: space, matter, and time. Each of these is divided into three. Space, for instance, is composed of length, breadth, and height, each separate and distinct in itself, yet the three are one. Length, breadth and height are not three spaces, but three dimensions comprising one space. Run enough lines lengthwise and you take in the whole. But so it is with the width and height. Each is separate and distinct, yet each is all of space—just as the Father, Son, and Holy Spirit is each God.

Time also is a trinity: past, present, and future—two invisible and one visible. Each is separate and distinct, yet each is the whole. Man himself is a trinity of spirit, soul, and body, two of which are invisible, one visible. Many more details could be given of the Godhead's trinity reflected in the universe. It can hardly be coincidence.

The Hebrew word *elohim* (gods) occurs about 2500 times in the Old Testament, while the singular form *(el)* occurs only 250 times and most of those designate false gods. Genesis 1:1 reads, "In the beginning, *elohim* created the heaven and the earth"; that is, literally, *"gods* created the heaven and the earth." Though a single noun is available, yet the plural form is consistently used for God. And in violation of grammatical rules, with few exceptions, singular verbs and pronouns are used with this plural noun. Why?

At the burning bush it was *elohim* (gods) who spoke to Moses. Yet *elohim* did not say, "We are that we are," but "I AM THAT I AM" (Exodus 3:14). One cannot escape the fact that, all through the Bible, God is presented as a plurality and yet as One, as having both diversity and unity. This is unique among all the world's religions! To reject the Trinity is to reject the God of the Bible.

The New Testament presents three Persons who are distinct, yet each is recognized as God. At the same time we have repeatedly the clear statement that there is only one true God. Christ prays to the Father. Is He praying to Himself? "The Father sent the Son to be the Saviour of the world" (1 John 4:14). Did He send Himself? Worse yet, did one "office" pray to and send a "title"? The Father, Son, and Holy Spirit each has distinct functions, yet each works only in conjunction with the others. Christ said, "The words that I speak unto you I speak not of myself [on my own initiative]: but the Father that dwelleth in me, he doeth the works" (John 14:10) and "I will pray the Father, and he shall give you another Comforter...even the Spirit of truth" (John 14:16,17). Throughout the New Testament, the Father, Son, and Holy Spirit are each separately honored and act as God, yet only in concert with one another.

The Old Testament also presents three Persons in the Godhead interacting. For example: "Hearken unto me, O Jacob and Israel, my called; I am he; I am the first, I also am the last. Mine hand also hath laid the foundation of the earth, and my right hand hath spanned the heavens...From the time that it was, there am I: and now the Lord God, and his Spirit, hath sent me" (Isaiah 48:12-16). The One speaking through Isaiah refers to Himself as "the first and the last" and the Creator of all, so He must be God. But He speaks of two others in the same passage who must also be God: "the Lord God, and his Spirit, hath sent me." Jesus presented a similar passage to the Pharisees (Matthew 22:41-46) when He asked them who the Messiah was, and they said, "The son of David." He then quoted, "The LORD said unto my Lord, Sit thou on my right hand, till I make thine enemies thy footstool" (Psalm 110:1). Then Jesus asked them, "If David then call him Lord, how is he his son?" The Pharisees were speechless. Unitarianism cannot explain these two "Lords."

It is a mystery how God can exist in three Persons yet be one God; but it is also a mystery how God could have no beginning and create everything out of nothing. We can't understand what a human soul or spirit is. Nor can we explain love or beauty or justice. It is beyond human capacity to comprehend the full nature of God's being. But neither can we understand what it means for us or anything else to exist—nor can we comprehend what space is or what time is or matter is. For every door science opens, there are ten more unopened doors on the other side. The more we learn, the more rapidly the unknown expands before us like receding images in a hall of mirrors. The Jehovah's Witnesses and other Unitarians argue that because the Trinity can't be understood it can't be true. But the fact that it is beyond human comprehension is no reason for rejecting what the Bible so consistently presents to us. God is telling us about Himself so we can believe in and know Him. We dare not reject what He says or lower it to the level of our finite minds.

Part of the mystery is the fact that if God did not exist as three Persons in One there could be no salvation. Only God could pay the infinite penalty for sin demanded by His infinite justice. All through the Old Testament the God of Israel whose name is *Jahweh (I AM THAT I AM)* declares not only that He is the only true God but that He is the only Saviour: "I, even I, am the LORD; and besides me there is no saviour...O God of Israel, the Saviour...Look unto me, and be ye saved, all the ends of the earth: for I am God, and there is none else...I the LORD am thy Saviour and thy Redeemer" (Isaiah 43:11; 45:15,22; 49:26; 60:16).

The New Testament, too, testifies that God is the Savior. The expression "God our Savior" is used repeatedly: 1 Timothy 1:1; 2:3; Titus 2:10; 3:4; Jude 25. But for God to pay the penalty for mankind's sins would itself not be just because He is not one of us. God would have to become a man in order to represent us in payment of sin. How could He do that and remain God in control of His universe? Only if God is three Persons yet One.

At the same time that it declares that God is the only Savior, the New Testament makes it equally clear that Jesus Christ is the Savior. The angel of the Lord tells Joseph in a dream that Mary, the virgin to whom he is engaged to be married, is with child of the Holy Spirit, that she will give birth to a son, and he instructs Joseph: "thou shalt call his name JESUS: for he shall save his people from their sins" (Matthew 1:21). Announcing the birth of Jesus to the shepards, the angel of the Lord tells them: "For unto you is born this day in the city of David a Saviour, which is Christ the Lord" (Luke 2:11). The expression "the Lord Jesus Christ our Saviour" or the equivalent is found repeatedly: Philippians 3:20; 2 Timothy 1:10; Titus 1:4. It follows, then, that Jesus must be God come to earth as a man through the virgin birth, and the New Testament declares that fact again and again: Titus 2:13, Jude 25.

In the Old Testament, after making it crystal clear that He alone is the Savior, God proceeds to introduce the One whom

He calls, "my servant" and reveals that He is to be the Savior of the world. Of Him God says, "that thou mayest be my salvation unto the end of the earth" (Isaiah 49:6). How is He to save the world from the penalty of sin? God, who is the only Savior, tells us through His prophet that His servant, who, it becomes clear, is the Messiah, must suffer and die for sin: "Behold my servant...his visage was so marred more than any man...He is despised and rejected...a man of sorrows... wounded for our transgression...bruised for our iniquities... he was cut off out of the land of the living: for the transgression of my people was he stricken...it pleased the LORD [Jahweh] to bruise him; he hath put him to grief: when thou shalt make his soul an offering for sin...shall my righteous servant justify many; for he shall bear their iniquities... because he hath poured out his soul unto death" (Isaiah 52:13,14; 53:3-13).

How can God be the only Savior, yet Jesus Christ is the only Savior? And how can God call the Savior His servant and punish Him for the sins of the world? This is only possible with the Trinity. John refers to Jesus Christ like this: "That which was from the beginning, which we have heard, which we have seen with our own eyes...and our hands have handled...that eternal life, which was with the Father...declare we unto you...And we have seen and do testify that the Father sent the Son to be the Saviour of the world" (1 John 1:1-3; 4:14).

The Father sent the Son! Isaiah had already prophesied this remarkable event: "For unto us a child is born [the babe in Bethlehem], unto us a son is given [the eternal Son of God]: and the government shall be upon his shoulder: and his name shall be called Wonderful, Counselor, The mighty God, The everlasting Father...of his Government and peace there shall be no end [He is the Messiah who is to rule Israel on David's throne]" (Isaiah 9:6,7). So the babe that is to be born in Bethlehem of a virgin is both man and "The mighty God," He is both the Son of God, yet He is also "The everlasting Father."

Jesus declared, "He that hath seen me hath seen the Father...I and my Father are one" (John 14:9; 10:30).

Only God could be and is the Savior; but His Servant, the Messiah, whom He sent to earth is the Savior. The Savior must be both God and man; and this is only possible because of the Trinity whereby the Father could send His Son, who is God and One with Him, to be the Savior of the world.

22

Understanding the Incarnation

And the Word was made flesh,
and dwelt among us....
—JOHN 1:14

Paul reminds us, "[G]reat is the mystery of godliness: God was manifest in the flesh, justified in the Spirit, seen of angels, preached unto the Gentiles, believed on in the world, received up into glory" (1 Timothy 3:16). What a mystery the incarnation is. How astonishing—and yet essential to our salvation—that God, as the Hebrew prophets in the Old Testament foretold (Isaiah 7:14; 9:6; Micah 5:2), could become a man. Nor did He, at His incarnation, cease to be God, which would be impossible. God and man now exist together in one Person, the Lord Jesus Christ, the unique God-man.

Mary, a virgin when Jesus was conceived and born, knew that God was His Father, but it was too much to understand. He nursed at her breast, grew as a child, and at night His rhythmic breathing mingled with that of the other sleeping children to whom Mary gave birth by Joseph (Matthew

> How incredible it is that God became a man; and how wonderful are the implications for us for eternity!

12:47; 13:55; Mark 3:32; Luke 8:20). So "normal" was He as a child that Mary lapsed by habit into calling Joseph His father—"thy father and I have sought thee sorrowing." When Jesus gently reproved her—"wist ye not that I must be about my Father's business"—she and Joseph "understood not" what He meant. Mary pondered this mystery "in her heart" (Luke 2:19,48-51).

Jesus was not popularly acclaimed in Nazareth. He was unrecognized and even hated "without a cause" (John 15:25). Here was God Himself, the Creator, walking among His creatures—and they despised Him. How deep was the alienation between God and man. Few were those who could say, "And the Word was made flesh, and dwelt among us, (and we beheld his glory, the glory as of the only begotten of the Father), full of grace and truth" (John 1:14).

The careful language of Scripture calls Christ "the *second* man" (1 Corinthians 15:47). From Adam until this One, there was no one who deserved to be truly called "man" in the fullness God purposed. As Adam was created by God, so Christ's body was created in the womb of a virgin: "A body hast thou prepared me" (Hebrews 10:5). Here was man once again as God had intended him to be. Here, too, was God as man: "He that hath seen me hath seen the Father" (John 14:9).

As the progenitor of a new race of those who have been born again, Christ is also called the *last* Adam (1 Corinthians 15:45). Those redeemed by His blood (Ephesians 1:7; Colossians 1:14), to whom He has given eternal life as a free gift of His grace, will "never perish" (John 10:28). Never will there be a third Adam or a fourth. What God accomplished in Christ for Adam's fallen descendants will never fail: "For by one offering [of Himself upon the cross for sin] he hath perfected for ever them that are sanctified" (Hebrews 10:14).

How incredible it is that God became a man; and how wonderful are the implications for us for eternity! As we have previously seen, God *had* to become a man to pay the penalty which His infinite justice required of man for sin: "Wherefore, as by one man sin entered into the world, and death by sin" (Romans 5:12), so it had to be that "by man came also the resurrection of the dead" (1 Corinthians 15:21).

The God of the Bible created the universe out of nothing. The universe is not God nor an extension of Him, nor is He part of it. Therefore, to speak of God as "She" or to refer to "Mother Earth" or "Mother Nature" or even "Mother/Father God" promotes a grave heresy. A woman nurtures her offspring within her womb and gives birth out of herself, precisely what God does not do. Nor is man, though in God's image (Genesis 1:26,27), an extension of God or part of God but a separate being entirely.

Obviously, being made "in the image of God" has nothing to do with man's physical form, for "God is a Spirit" (John 4:24). Man was made in the spiritual and moral image of God. God made man's body from the "dust of the ground." Man's soul and spirit, however, are nonphysical: "And the LORD God...breathed into his [Adam's] nostrils the breath of life; and man became a living soul" (Genesis 2:7). Reflecting the triune nature of God (Father, Son, and Holy Spirit), man is also a triune being: body, soul, and spirit. Paul wrote, "I pray God your whole spirit and soul and body be preserved blameless unto the coming of our Lord Jesus Christ" (1 Thessalonians 5:23). God's Word causes a "dividing asunder of soul and spirit" (Hebrews 4:12). Having made man a triune being in His image, God could become a man in order to redeem His creatures.

At first, the Spirit of God indwelt the spirits of Adam and Eve. Their focus was toward God. The enjoyment of bodily pleasures and sense of their own identities was more wonderful than we can imagine because it was all to the glory of God rather than for self-gratification. When they sinned, the Spirit of God departed from their spirits and their orientation turned from God to self. Thus we, their descendants, are by nature sensual, selfish, and materialistic. Instead of the joy of fellowship with God, man finds his joy in this world's "lust of the flesh, and the lust of the eyes, and the pride of life" (1 John 2:16).

These three lusts are all that Satan and the world have to offer. We see them in Eve's sin: the forbidden fruit's delicious taste, its enticing visual appeal, and the wisdom with which it would endow her (Genesis 3:1-6). We see them in Satan's tempting of Christ: to turn stones into bread to satisfy His bodily hunger; to succumb to the appealing panorama of "all the kingdoms of the world, and the glory of them"; and to cast Himself from the pinnacle of the temple, causing the angels to catch Him in midair and the watching Jews to worship Him (Matthew 4:1-11). Unlike the first man and first Adam, the Second Man and Last Adam refused Satan's offer.

In everyone else except Christ, the unique God-Man, the battle rages between man's flesh and God's Spirit: "For the flesh lusteth against the Spirit, and the Spirit against the flesh" (Galatians 5:17). Even Paul acknowledged, "For the good that I would I do not: but the evil which I would not, that I do" (Romans 7:19). Man's spirit has become a slave to his soul and body. He can never be right—even his morality and uprightness can never be anything but the "filthy rags" (Isaiah 64:6) of self-righteousness—until the Spirit of God indwells and rules in man's spirit once again. Only Christ, in whose person God and man have been united, can bring this reconciliation within man's heart. Paul, who said, "O wretched man that I am! Who shall deliver me from the body of this death?" declared in triumph, "I thank God [that there is deliverance] through Jesus Christ our Lord" (Romans 7:24,25)!

David exulted, "I am fearfully and wonderfully made" (Psalm 139:14). Materialism has trivialized man. Materialistic science has denied the nonphysical spirit and soul of man and turned him into a stimulus-response mechanism. It alleges that man's thoughts, ambitions, likes, dislikes, even his sense of right and wrong and the experience of love and compassion, can all be explained in terms of electrical and chemical impulses in his brain and nervous system. Such folly was the basis for Sigmund Freud's theories and is still behind the treatment of mental disorders with drugs.

Yes, the brain may be like a computer, but no computer can think on its own. Someone must tell it what to do. What folly to imagine that thoughts originate in the brain. If so, as we earlier pointed out, we would be prisoners of our brains, helplessly dragged along as its chemical/electrical processes determined our thoughts and even our morals and emotions. In fact, thought is initiated by the soul and spirit, which use the brain to operate the body and to interface with this physical world of sensual experience in which our bodies function.

There are more cells in the brain than stars in the universe, and these cells make up hundreds of billions of neurons and trillions of synapses in perfect balance. Moreover, the mysterious link between the spirit of man, made in God's image, and his brain and body is forever beyond the grasp of science. Yet that connection is being tampered with by drugs in order to adjust man's behavior—behavior which was meant to reflect God's perfect purity, but instead reflects man's rebellion and sin as a child of Satan: "Ye are of your father, the devil" (John 8:44). There are no *chemical* solutions to spiritual problems. Yet millions take drugs such as Prozac, Effexor, Valium, Ritalin, Zoloft, Paxil, and so on to deal with spiritual problems.

The Bible declares that man's inner turmoil, insecurity, lust, anger, conflict with himself and others, and any other "emotional problems" which beset him are spiritual at their root (2 Corinthians 7:1; Galatians 5:16; Colossians 1:21). They result from man's rebellion against God and the wrenching separation from God which that rebellion effected in the depths of his being. Therefore, the solution to man's emotional and spiritual problems is reconciliation to God. Tragically, that solution is being set aside in favor of correcting a "chemical imbalance" in the brain with drugs.

There is no doubt much that can go wrong with the brain as a *physical* instrument, such as nutritional deficiency or various traumas. However, even secular psychiatrists admit that the brain is far too complex to be precisely "adjusted" with drugs.

> His incarnation united God and man in His own person; and He brings that reconciliation and union within the human spirit when He is received as Savior and invited to dwell there.

The awesome implications of tampering with the brain are not generally recognized by those relying upon chemical solutions. Nor are Christian psychologists acknowledging the even more serious consequences of tampering with the brain's response to the soul and spirit of man, so "fearfully and wonderfully" made in the image of God.

A word of caution: We are not advocating that anyone now taking medication should stop abruptly. Psychiatric drugs can be addictive, and to stop suddenly could have serious consequences. *Any* change in medication should be only under the supervision of a physician. We are simply pointing out that no one really knows how drugs work or the full range of their effects. Many drugs prescribed by physicians for years have only later been found to have such devastating effects that they have been removed from the market.

The connection between the spirit and the brain and body is known only to God. The *moral* and *spiritual* consequences of tampering with the brain and nervous system through drugs could be far worse than the *physical* dangers. Consider depression, for example. Drugs too often mask the real need and hinder one from turning to Christ for the spiritual solution that can only be found in Him. In pursuing a chemical solution, science ignores (because it cannot deal with it) what ought to be the first priority: getting right with God through the redemption which is in the Lord Jesus

Christ alone. His incarnation united God and man in His own person; and He brings that reconciliation and union within the human spirit when He is received as Savior and invited to dwell there. Christianity (unlike Hinduism, Buddhism, Islam) is not a set of rules for one to follow in one's own strength. Only Christ can live the Christian life, and He will live it in and through those who believe in Him. Note the wonder of what Paul said: "[I]t pleased God...to reveal his Son in me" (Galatians 1:15,16). He wants to reveal His Son in us as well. That's what Christianity is.

The indwelling of Christ within the human spirit is as great a mystery as the Incarnation itself. To those who trust Him and obey His Word, He becomes their very life: "I am crucified with Christ: nevertheless I live; yet not I, but Christ liveth in me" (Galatians 2:20); "ye are dead, and your life is hid with Christ in God" (Colossians 3:3).

Obviously, the Spirit of Christ within needs no help from psychotherapy or drugs. What we need above all is to trust, obey, and rejoice in Him. Nor does Christ promise an easy path. The Christian life is beset by trials and temptations and conflicts between the flesh and the Spirit, allowed by God to test us to see whether or not we will really trust and obey Him. As He told Israel,

> And thou shalt remember all the way which the LORD thy God led thee these forty years in the wilderness, to humble thee, and to prove thee, to know what was in thine heart, whether thou wouldest keep his commandments, or no. And he humbled thee, and suffered thee to hunger...that he might make thee know that man doth not live by bread only, but by every word that proceedeth out of the mouth of the LORD doth man live (Deuteronomy 8:2,3).

Without the incarnation, mankind was doomed eternally. "All have sinned, and come short of the glory of God" (Romans 3:23); and "The wages of sin is death; but the gift of God is eternal life through Jesus Christ our Lord" (Romans

6:23). We believe in Christ as our Savior from the *penalty* of sin. Let us also trust Him fully as the One who indwells us and will *overcome* sin in our lives. May we rejoice in "the riches of the glory of this mystery...Christ in you, the hope of glory" (Colossians 1:27)!

23

Understanding the Church

*"I will build my church; and the gates of hell shall
not prevail against it."*
—MATTHEW 16:18

Christ was born "King of the Jews" (Matthew 2:2), was
called "King of Israel" and "King of the Jews" (Matthew
27:11; Mark 15:2), and acknowledged both titles (John
1:49,50; 12:12-15). He did not renounce His claim to David's
throne even though His own people (as the prophets had
foretold) "despised, rejected" (Isaiah 53:3), and crucified
Him (Psalm 22:12-18; Isaiah 53:5,8-10; Zechariah 12:10). All
four Gospels declare that "King of the Jews" was the accusa-
tion placed on the cross (Matthew 27:37; Mark 15:26; Luke
23:38; John 19:19). Here is Mark's account of Israel rejecting
her King and demanding His crucifixion:

> But Pilate answered them, saying, Will ye that I
> release unto you the King of the Jews?...
> But the chief priests moved the people, that he
> should rather release Barabbas unto them.

> And Pilate answered and said again unto them,
> What will ye then that I shall do unto him whom
> ye call the King of the Jews?
> And they cried out again, Crucify him. (Mark
> 15:9-13)

The Hebrew prophets had foretold that Christ would rise from the dead and that He would come again to establish a kingdom that would never end (1 Kings 2:45; Isaiah 9:7; Daniel 7:14). Christ has fulfilled only the first part, rising from the dead and ascending to the Father's right hand. If the remainder of those prophecies is to be fulfilled (and they must be, or God has lied) there must be a future restoration of the kingdom to Israel as the disciples believed (Acts 1:6), as Peter affirmed (Acts 3:19-26), and as Christ acknowledged (Acts 1:6,7). Israel's future repentance, redemption, and restoration are foretold often (Ezekiel 36–39; Zechariah 12–14; Acts 5:31). Paul prayed for Israel's salvation (Romans 10:1) and declared that "all Israel shall be saved" (Romans 11:26).

> Both the Gentile and the Jew who enter the church through faith in Christ are thereafter under a higher law, "the law of the Spirit of life in Christ Jesus."
> —Romans 8:2

If the Muslims and other nations in the world would understand these prophecies concerning Israel's right to her land and honor them and the God who gave them, there would be peace in the Middle East and throughout the world. Instead, they will persist in their desire to destroy Israel, resulting in Christ's intervention from heaven to rescue Israel at Armageddon and to destroy Antichrist, his followers, and his kingdom. Most Israelis themselves do not believe that God gave them their land. They are trading God's land (Leviticus 25:23) for a fool's "peace" with an enemy who has sworn to exterminate them.

Knowing that Israel would reject and crucify Him, Christ said He would build a new entity, the church. This would occur in the interim prior to Israel's restoration while "Jerusalem shall be trodden down of the Gentiles, until the times of Gentiles be fulfilled" (Luke 21:24). The word "church" or "churches" (*ekklesia* in Greek, meaning "called out"), occurs about 114 times in the New Testament. No Hebrew word in the Old Testament is translated "church" in the King James version. Pertaining to Israel, the major comparable words in Hebrew are *edah, mowed,* and *qahal,* translated as "assembly" or "congregation." While Acts 7:38 refers to "the church [congregation of Israel] in the wilderness," the Bible makes a clear distinction between Israel and the New Testament church. The latter consists of both Jews and Gentiles and did not exist before Christ's death and resurrection. He continues to build that church even now. It was established by Him and specifically for Him: "*I* will build *my* church; and the gates of hell shall not prevail against it" (Matthew 16:18).

Here we have an obvious claim by Christ that He is God. Israel had been chosen by God. Who, then, but God Himself, could establish another congregation of believers in addition

> In the church, "There is neither Jew nor Greek [Gentile]... [but all are] one in Christ."
> —Galatians 3:28

to and distinct from Israel? Christ's statement regarding the church is similar to what He said to the Jews who "believed on him," and it has the same awesome implications: "If ye continue in *my* word, then are ye *my* disciples indeed; and ye shall know the truth, and the truth shall make you free" (John 8:31,32).

The Jews must have been stunned by that declaration. How could this one dare to use such terms as "*my* word" and "*my* disciples" and claim to set His followers free? Was it not *God's* Word they were to follow, and were they not *Moses'* disciples? Was He claiming to be greater than Moses—even equal to God? Whatever it meant to be His disciple, He was obviously starting something new.

Nevertheless, no one imagined that this miracle worker intended to dispense with Israel and replace her with some other entity. Nor did Christ ever imply, much less say, that He would do so. That misunderstanding arose much later and still persists. The belief that the church replaces Israel remains today among Roman Catholics, among those of Reformed theology such as Presbyterians and Lutherans, and among many charismatics as well.

In its infancy, the church was composed only of Jewish believers. They had difficulty believing that Gentiles, too, could be saved through Christ and be in the church, even though the Old Testament prophets had laid that foundation (Psalm 72:11; Isaiah 11:10; 42:1-6; Malachi 1:11). And even when they understood the "mystery" revealed by Paul "that the Gentiles should be fellow heirs, and of the same body, and partakers of his promise in Christ by the gospel" (Ephesians 3:3-6), some of them tried to subject the Gentiles to the Jewish law. In effect, they were erroneously making the church an extension of Israel (Acts 15:1).

Gentiles are "aliens from the commonwealth of Israel, and strangers from the covenants of promise" (Ephesians 2:12). When a Gentile is saved and is added by Christ as a "living stone" to the church under construction (1 Peter 2:5), he doesn't come under the Jewish laws and customs of the old covenant. And when a Jew is saved and added to the church, he is set free from the Jewish law (the "law of sin and death") and its penalties (Romans 8:1). Both the Gentile and the Jew who enter the church through faith in Christ are thereafter under a higher law, "the law of the Spirit of life in Christ Jesus" (Romans 8:2). Indeed, Christ has become their life, living out through them this new standard of holy conduct—something that was unknown in Israel even to her greatest prophets (1 Peter 1:10-12).

Paul describes the church as "an holy temple in the Lord" still under construction: "In whom ye also are builded together for an habitation of God through the Spirit" (Ephesians 2:21,22).

No one can establish himself in that sacred temple; he must be placed there by Christ alone. The living stones which He is building together to form the eternal temple do not fall in and out of the structure. We are *in Christ* and eternally secure.

The church is Christ's body, nourished by Him. Believers are spoken of as branches in the true vine, depicting a continual flow of life and nourishment from Him to them. Christ is the head of the body, which is therefore directed by Him and not by a priesthood or hierarchy of men in some earthly headquarters. The headquarters of the church is in heaven. Yet today's denominations (like the cults) all have their earthly headquarters and their traditions. They have become organizations instead of being content with being part of the organism, His body.

In the church, "There is neither Jew nor Greek [Gentile]... [but all are] one in Christ" (Galatians 3:28). Gentiles do not become Jewish nor do Jews become Gentiles, but Jew and Gentile have become "one *new* man" (Ephesians 2:15). Through the cross, Christ "abolished" the "ordinances" which had separated Jew and Gentile. Therefore, we can confidently affirm that Gentiles are not to adopt those ordinances. Would one of Christ's own adopt something which God has abolished?

Paul's epistle to the Galatians was written to correct the error of salvation partly through Christ and partly through works. In all of his epistles, Paul comes back to the theme that salvation is all of grace and nothing of works. Herein is a major difference between Israel and the church; for the former, eternal life was promised to those who kept the law (which no one could do); for the latter, eternal life comes by grace through faith.

The old covenant offered life to the righteous who kept the law: "this do and thou shalt live" (Deuteronomy 8:1; Luke 10:28). But no one could live up to that standard, for "all have sinned" (Romans 3:23). Under the new covenant (Jeremiah 31:31-34), "to him that worketh not, but believeth on him that justifieth the ungodly, his faith is counted for righteousness" (Romans 4:5). Human pride insists upon becoming righteous on its own—an impossible task. Though the nation of Israel as a whole will not realize the benefits of the new covenant until the Second Coming, God's grace in salvation has been available to all by faith from Adam onward.

Paul mourned the fact that his people Israel, though they had "a zeal after God" yet "they being ignorant of God's righteousness, and going about to establish their own righteousness, have not submitted themselves unto the righteousness of God" (Romans 10:3) through the new covenant. So it is with all the cults. It is the error of the Pharisee who proclaimed his righteousness to God and was not heard, whereas the publican, who acknowledged his unworthiness, was justified (Luke 18:10-14).

One had to belong to Israel (with some exceptions) to be saved; but one must be saved (with no exceptions) in order to belong to the church. The church is not a vehicle of salvation. Making that claim is a major error of most cults. Each claims salvation comes through their church. In fact, salvation is for those outside the true church and only then can one become a part of it.

Salvation has always been and still is the same for both Jew and Gentile; but God's plans for Israel are different from His plans for the church. Jews (like Gentiles) who believe in Christ prior to His Second Coming (when He makes Himself known to Israel in rescuing her in the midst of Armageddon and all Israel is saved) are in the church. Jews who only come to faith in Christ at Armageddon will continue into the millennial kingdom on earth and Christ will reign over them from the throne of David. Many Gentiles will be saved at that time also, but "*all* Israel shall be saved" (Romans 11:26).

The Galatian problem remains (in varying degrees) within some so-called Hebrew-Christian or Messianic congregations today. There is often a tendency to imagine that a return to Jewish customs (even by Gentiles) makes for greater sanctity. Extrabiblical traditions are honored, for example, in the seder ceremony at Passover, as though inspired of God. Scripture alone must be our guide, to the exclusion of manmade traditions, which Christ condemned (Matthew 15:1-9; Mark 7:9-13), as did the apostles (Galatians 1:13,14; Colossians 2:8; 1 Peter 1:18). Traditions developed over the centuries have led to great error within both Catholicism and Protestantism.

We must ever remember that Christ intended the church to be something new and separate from Israel. It would neither partake of nor interfere with God's promises to His earthly people, promises which will be fulfilled in their time. The church would be separate, too, from Israel's religious ordinances. Here, again, the cults have gone astray.

Mormonism, for example, pretends to have both an Aaronic and Melchisedec priesthood. On the contrary, in the church every believer is a priest (1 Peter 2:9) and the sacrifices offered are "praise to God continually, that is, the fruit of our lips giving thanks to his name" and "to do good" (Hebrews 13:15,16).

In fact, there are no longer any propitiatory sacrifices offered for the forgiveness of sins because the church was made possible by the one sacrifice of Christ upon the cross. That sacrifice is never to be repeated because it paid the full penalty demanded by God's justice and made it possible for God to "be just, and the justifier of him which believeth in Jesus" (Romans 3:26). Consequently, "there is no more offering for sin" (Hebrews 10:18). The grave error of the "sacrifice of the Eucharist" or the Mass is in the claim that Christ is still being "immolated" in sacrifice for sin.

Israel broke the covenant God made with her. She demonstrated that "by the deeds of the law there shall no flesh be justified in his sight: for by the law is the knowledge of sin" (Romans 3:20). Her sacrificial system could not take away sin, but looked forward to the unique "Lamb of God, which taketh away the sin of the world" (John 1:29). The establishment of a "new covenant" with Israel (Jeremiah 31:31) is foretold. Animal sacrifices had opened the way for the Jewish high priest into the earthly sanctuary which was patterned after the heavenly reality (Hebrews 9:1-10). When Christ died on the cross, "the veil of the temple was rent in twain from the top to the bottom" (Mark 15:38), ending the animal sacrifices. Now we have a "great high priest, that is passed into the heavens, Jesus the Son of God" (Hebrews 4:14), who, "by his own blood...obtained eternal redemption for us" (Hebrews 9:12).

Israel was given a land on earth (Genesis 12:1; 15:18-21; 17:7,8), her destiny is tied to it, and she will never cease to exist there (Jeremiah 31:35-40). Numerous prophecies promise her restoration to her land, with the Messiah, upon His return, ruling her from the throne of David (Isaiah 9:6,7; Ezekiel 37:24,25; Luke 1:31-33). The promise is clear that God will pour out His Spirit upon His chosen people, after which they will never pollute His holy name again and He will never again hide His holy face from Israel (Ezekiel 39:7,27-29; Zechariah 13,14).

Israel must endure forever (Jeremiah 31:35-38) or the prophecies of the Bible and Christ's promises to her could not be fulfilled. Christ referred to the cities of Israel in existence at His Second Coming (Matthew 10:23), proof enough that the church has not replaced her. As further proof (though not needed), Christ promised His disciples that they would rule over "the twelve tribes of Israel" with Him in His millennial kingdom (Matthew 19:28; Luke 22:30).

The church cannot fulfill the prophecies to Israel, never having belonged to a specific land nor having been cast out of it or returned to it. Rather, the church comes "out of every kindred, and tongue, and people, and nation" (Revelation 5:9). The hope of the church is to be raptured to heaven (John 14:3; 1 Thessalonians 4:16,17), where we stand before "the judgment seat of Christ" (Romans 14:10; 2 Corinthians 5:10) and then are married to our Lord (Revelation 19:7-9) and are eternally with Him wherever He is (John 14:3; 1 Thessalonians 4:17).

That being the case, in love with our Bridegroom and longing to see Him face to face, let us hold the things of earth lightly and live for eternity. Let us please Him alone, not following men or organizations, but by faith allowing our Head to nourish, sustain, and direct us and to live His life through us to His glory.

24

Eternally Secure

*These things have I written unto you that believe
on the name of the Son of God; that ye may know
that ye have eternal life....*
—1 JOHN 5:13

The question of the eternal security of the believer has been the cause of much controversy in the church for centuries and still creates confusion and distress for many Christians.

Those who believe in "falling away" accuse those who believe in "eternal security" of promoting "cheap grace." The latter is in itself an unbiblical expression. To call it "cheap" is really a denial of grace, since it implies that too small a price has been paid. Grace, however, must be absolutely free and without any price at all *on man's part*, while *on God's part* the price He paid must be infinite. Thus for man to think that his works can play any part in either earning or keeping his salvation is what cheapens grace and devalues this infinite gift to the level of human effort.

To speak of "falling from grace" involves the same error. Since our works had nothing to do with meriting grace in the first place, there is nothing we could do that would cause us to no longer merit it and thus to "fall" from it. Works determine reward or punishment—not one's salvation, which comes by God's grace. The crux of the problem is a confusion about grace and works.

First of all, we must be absolutely clear that these two can never mix. Paul declares, "If by grace, then is it no more of works: otherwise grace is no more grace. But if it be of works, then is it no more grace, otherwise work is no more work" (Romans 11:6). Salvation cannot be partly by works and partly by grace. These two are opposites and cannot be in partnership.

Secondly, we must be absolutely certain that works have nothing to do with salvation. Period. The Bible clearly states, "For by *grace* are ye saved...*not of works*" (Ephesians 2:8,9). True to such scriptures, evangelicals firmly declare that we cannot earn or merit salvation *in any way*. Eternal life must be received as a free gift of God's grace, or we cannot have it, for "the gift of God is eternal life" (Romans 6:23). Any attempt at even a partial payment for a gift is a rejection of the gift.

Thirdly, salvation cannot be purchased *even in part* by us because it requires payment of the penalty for sin—a payment we can't make. If one receives a speeding ticket, it won't help to say to the judge, "I've driven many times within the 55 mph limit. Surely my many good deeds will make up for the one bad deed." Nor will it do to say, "If you let me off this time, I promise never to break the law again." The judge would reply, "Never to break the law again is only to do what the law demands. You get no extra credit for that. The penalty for breaking the law is a separate matter and must be paid." Thus Paul writes, "By the deeds of the law there shall no flesh be justified in his sight" (Romans 3:20).

Fourthly, if salvation from the penalty of breaking God's laws cannot be earned by good deeds, then it cannot be lost by bad deeds. Our works play no part in either earning or keeping salvation. If we had to merit keeping the gift, it would not be a gift.

Fifthly, salvation can only be given to us as a free gift if the penalty has been fully paid. We have violated infinite justice, requiring an infinite penalty. We are finite beings and could not pay it; we would be separated from God for eternity. God is infinite and could pay an infinite penalty, but it wouldn't be just, because He is not a member of our race. Therefore God, in love and grace, through the virgin birth, became a man so that He could pay the debt of sin for the entire human race.

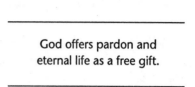

God offers pardon and eternal life as a free gift.

In the Greek, *tetelestai*, Christ's cry from the cross, "It is finished!" is an accounting term. In Christ's day, it was stamped upon invoices and promissory notes as proof of full satisfaction. Christ thus declared that the sinner's debt to divine justice had been paid in full. Justice had been satisfied by full payment of its penalty, and thus God could "be just, and the justifier of him which believeth in Jesus" (Romans 3:26). On that basis, God offers pardon and eternal life as a free gift. He cannot force it upon anyone or it would not be a gift. Nor would it be just to pardon a person who rejects the righteous basis for pardon and offers a hopelessly inadequate payment instead—or offers his works even as partial payment.

Salvation is the full pardon by grace from the penalty of all sin, past, present, or future; eternal life is the bonus thrown in. Denying this cardinal truth, all cultists, such as Jehovah's Witnesses and Mormons, for example, reject salvation by grace and insist that it must be earned by one's good works. They accuse evangelicals of teaching that all we need to do is to say we believe in Christ and then we can live as we please, even in the grossest of sins, yet be sure of heaven. Evangelicals don't teach that at all, yet a similar complaint is made by those who believe in "falling away." They say that "once saved, always saved" encourages one to live in sin because if we know we cannot be lost then we have no incentive for living a holy life. On the contrary, love for the One who saved us is the greatest and only acceptable motive for living a holy life; and surely the greater the salvation one has received, the more love and gratitude there will be. So to know one is secure for eternity gives a higher motive for living a good life than the fear of losing one's salvation if one sins.

While those who believe in "falling from grace" are clear that good works cannot *earn* salvation, they teach that salvation is *kept* by good works. Thus one gets saved by grace, but thereafter salvation can be lost by works. To teach that good works keep salvation is almost the same error as to say that good works earn salvation. It denies grace to say that once I have been saved by grace I must thereafter keep myself saved by works.

If those who are saved could lose their salvation, then they must by their own actions keep themselves saved. If that is true, then those who stay saved and get to heaven will be able to boast that they played a key role in their salvation. Christ saved them but they kept themselves saved. On the contrary, no man can take any credit for his salvation. We are "kept by the power of God" (1 Peter 1:5), not by our faith or efforts.

According to Hebrews 6:4-9, the "falling away" doctrine, rather than glorifying Christ, once again holds Him up to shame and ridicule before the world for two reasons: if we could lose our salvation, then 1) Christ would have to be crucified again to save us again; and 2) He would be ridiculed for dying to *purchase* a salvation but not making adequate provision to *preserve* it—for giving a priceless gift to those who would inevitably lose it. If Christ's death in our place for our sins and His resurrection were not sufficient to keep us saved, then He has foolishly wasted His time. If we could not live a good enough life to earn salvation, it is certain we cannot live a good enough life to keep it. To make the salvation He procured ultimately dependent upon our faltering works would be the utmost folly.

"Falling away" doctrine makes us worse off after we are saved than before. At least before conversion we can get saved. But after we are saved and have lost our salvation (if we could), we can't get saved again, but are lost forever. Hebrews 6:6 declares, "*If* (not *when*) they shall fall away...*it is impossible*...to renew them again unto repentance." That "falling away" is hypothetical is clear (verse 9): "But, beloved, we are persuaded better things of you, and things that accompany salvation, though we thus speak." So "falling away" does not "accompany salvation." The writer is showing us that if we could lose our salvation, we could never get it back without Christ dying again upon the cross. This is folly. He would have to die an infinite number of times (that is, every time every person who was once saved sinned and was lost and wanted to be "saved again"). Thus, those who reject "once saved, always saved" can only replace it with "once lost, always lost."

John assures us, "These things have I written unto you that believe on the name of the Son of God; that ye may know [present knowledge] that ye have [present possession] eternal life..." (1 John 5:13). If the person who had eternal life could lose it and suffer eternal death, to call it eternal life would be a mockery. On the contrary, eternal life is linked with the promise that one *cannot* perish—a clear assurance of "eternal security" or "once saved, always saved." John 3:16 promises those who believe in Jesus Christ that they "shall not perish, but have everlasting life." John 5:24 again says, "he that heareth my word, and believeth on him that sent me, hath everlasting life, and shall not come into condemnation." One could not ask for clearer or greater assurance than the words of Jesus: "I give unto them [My sheep] eternal life and they shall never perish" (John 10:28).

If sin causes the loss of salvation, what kind or amount of sin does it take? There is no verse in the Bible that tells us. We are told that "if we confess our sins, he is faithful and just to forgive us our sins and to cleanse us from all unrighteousness" (1 John 1:9)—so apparently any sin can be forgiven. Even those who teach falling away rarely if ever say they got "saved again." Rather, they confessed their sin and were forgiven. Hebrews 12:3-11 tells us that every Christian sins, and that instead of causing a loss of salvation, sin brings God's chastening upon us as His children. If when we sinned we ceased to be God's children, He would have no one to chastise—yet He "scourgeth every son whom he receiveth." Indeed, chastening is a sign that we are God's children, not that we have lost our salvation: "If ye be without chastisement, whereof all are partakers, then are ye bastards, and not sons."

Some teach that one must be baptized to be saved, others that one must "speak in tongues." Both are forms of salvation by works. Some people lack assurance of salvation because they haven't "spoken in tongues," others are confident they are saved because they think they have. Both are like those who say, "Lord, Lord, have we not...in thy name done many wonderful works?" (Matthew 7:21-23). They are relying on their works to prove they are saved instead of upon God's grace. Nor does Jesus say to these workers of signs and wonders, "You were once saved but lost your salvation." He says, "I *never* knew you." These are solemn words from the lips of Him who said, "I know my sheep" (John 10:14). If He *never* knew them, they were *never* His sheep.

Here is an important distinction. Those who believe in falling away would say of a professing Christian who has denied the faith and is living in unrepentant sin that he has "fallen from grace" and has "lost his salvation." In contrast, those who believe in eternal security, while no more tolerant of such conduct, would say of the same person that probably Christ "never knew him"—he was never a Christian. We must give the comfort and assurance of Scripture to those who are saved; but at the same time we must not give false and unbiblical comfort to those who merely say they are saved but deny with their lives what they profess with their lips.

Are we not then saved by our works? Indeed not. Every Christian's works are tried by fire at the "judgment seat of

Christ" before which "we must all appear" (2 Corinthians 5:10). Good works bring rewards; a lack of them does not cause loss of salvation. The person who hasn't even one good work (*all* of his works are burned up) is still "saved; yet so as by fire" (1 Corinthians 3:13-15). We would not think such a person was saved at all. Yet one who may seem outwardly not to be a Christian, who has no good works as evidence—if he has truly received the Lord Jesus Christ as his Savior, is then "saved as by fire" and shall never perish in spite of his lack of works. This is not theory or wishful thinking but what Paul clearly says under the inspiration of the Holy Spirit.

Do we then, on the basis of "once saved, always saved," encourage Christians to "sin that grace may abound"? With Paul we say, "God forbid!" We offer no comfort or assurance to those living in sin. We don't say, "You're okay because you once made a 'decision for Christ.'" Instead we warn, "If you are not willing right now to live fully for Christ as Lord of your life, how can you say that you were really sincere when you supposedly committed yourself to Him at some time in the past?" And to all, we declare with Paul, "Examine yourselves, whether ye be in the faith; prove your own selves" (2 Corinthians 13:5).

> Our confidence for eternity rests in His unchanging love and grace and the sufficiency of God's provision in Christ.

Our confidence for eternity rests in His unchanging love and grace and the sufficiency of God's provision in Christ—not in our worth or performance. Only when this is clear do we have real peace with God. Only then can we truly love Him and live for Him out of gratitude for the eternal life He has given to us as a free gift of His grace—a gift He will not take back and which He makes certain can never be lost!

25

Are We Living in the Last Days?

This know also, that in the last days perilous times shall come.
—1 TIMOTHY 3:1

How near to the end of time are we living today, or is it possible to tell? Unfortunately, there have always been enthusiasts who were convinced that they knew exactly when the end would come and who were able to persuade a multitude of followers to sell or give away their possessions and perch in trees or stand on hilltops to await the Second Coming. Apocalyptic theories flourish at the turn of every century, and especially at the end of a millennium.

Skeptics argue that the early Christians and even the apostles, as well as countless others down through the centuries, all thought they were living in the last days, and that the term is therefore meaningless. It is true that in his sermon on the Day of Pentecost (Acts 2:17) Peter seemed to apply an Old Testament prophecy about the "last days" (Joel 2:28-32) to the outpouring of the Spirit upon the disciples at that time. However, reading carefully the context in Joel along with

Peter's words makes it clear that Peter was not declaring that what was happening at that moment was the *fulfillment* of Joel's promise. Rather, it was a *sample* of what could have occurred if Israel had repented of her rejection of Christ: She could have experienced the millennial reign of her Messiah that Joel went on to describe. It was an offer that Israel refused (as it had been prophesied she would) but which she will accept at a future time, after God's judgment has been fully and finally visited upon her.

The apostle John, writing in about A.D. 95, declared: "Little children, it is the last time; and as ye have heard that antichrist shall come, even now are there many antichrists, whereby we know that it is the last time" (1 John 2:18). Yet John was by no means declaring that the "last days" had fully come, as some assert. He made it clear that although there were already many antichrists, *the Antichrist* was to appear at a future time.

> The New Testament writers seem to have understood the "last days" as a time that began with the ascension of Christ and would culminate with His Second Coming.

Let us be reminded that the rapture could always have occurred at any moment. Indeed, then as now, the early church was watching and waiting in eager anticipation of being taken to heaven in that glorious event. There are no explicit signs to indicate that the rapture is about to occur. The "last-days signs" are not for the church, but for an unbelieving Israel. Nothing stands between the church and that "blessed hope" of being caught up to meet her Bridegroom in the air.

Those events that Christ prophesied when He was asked for signs of His coming are intended to warn Israel of Antichrist's appearance and that, after guaranteeing her peace, he would seek to destroy her. The signs also herald the coming of Israel's Messiah to rescue her from Antichrist's attacking armies, an event which Christians refer to as Christ's Second Coming in power and glory. Since the rapture comes first, however, certain signs that indicate the nearness of the Second Coming may cast their shadows far enough in advance to tell the church that the rapture must be soon. Nevertheless, we are always, regardless of any signs, to expect the rapture to occur at any moment and to live in that expectancy.

As for the Second Coming, it would have been premature for Israel to expect it when only a few of the signs were in evidence. Jesus declared: "When ye shall see *all* these things, know that it [the Second Coming] is near, even at the doors" (Matthew 24:33). Israel has been alerted so that she might know exactly when the moment of her Messiah's intervention to save her has come. How many of these signs will cast their shadows before them at the time of the rapture no one can say. We do know, however, that our generation is the first for which *any* of these shadows have appeared, and we now have *many*.

The New Testament writers seem to have understood the "last days" as a time that began with the ascension of Christ and would culminate with His Second Coming. That event would be preceded by specific signs indicating that the generation on earth at that time was living in the *last* of the "last days." It is exciting to note that no generation has ever had solid biblical reason for believing that it was living in the *last* of the last days preceding the Second Coming of Christ—no generation until ours.

Why could our generation as opposed to all previous ones be living in the *last* of the last days? Because so many of the major signs the Bible gives to warn of the nearness of Christ's Second Coming could not possibly have applied in the past, but have only recently become applicable. For the first time in history all of the signs heralding the Second Coming could occur at any moment. In fact, the present generation—unlike any generation before it—has more than sufficient reason for believing that the Second Coming is very near.

What are these signs that have recently become viable for the first time in history? Jesus gave a number of them. For example, in speaking of the events that would precede His Second Coming, He warned of a time of unprecedented destruction which would be so severe that "except those days should be shortened, there should no flesh be saved..." (Matthew 24:22). Such a statement was a puzzle to past generations: How could the destruction of all life on earth be threatened through bows and arrows, swords and spears, or even the conventional weapons of World War II? Our generation, however, has developed and stockpiled arms unknown in the past and which actually have the potential to destroy all life on this planet. So we are the *first generation in history* for whom this particular prophecy no longer awaits some future development to make it possible.

In the vision of the future given to Him by Christ, John saw a world ruler controlling the whole earth not only politically and militarily, but economically. No one would be able to buy or sell without Antichrist's mysterious "666" stamp of approval embedded in his hand or forehead to indicate his loyalty to him (Revelation 13:16-18). While past generations took this threat seriously, there was no way that all commerce and banking on earth could be controlled from a central location. Today there is. We have the computers, communication satellites, and worldwide electronic banking networks which make such control feasible. Moreover, everyone knows that it is only a matter of time until such a system will be in place and enforced.

John also saw that the entire world would worship Satan along with the Antichrist: "And they worshiped the dragon [that old serpent the devil, or Satan—(12:9)] which gave power unto the beast [Antichrist]; and they worshiped the beast" (Revelation 13:4). Such a prophecy would have seemed unbelievable to previous generations, but not so in our day. Hard-core satanism has been called "the fastest-growing subculture among America's teens." Satanists have their own chaplains in the U.S. Armed Forces and are protected under freedom-of-religion laws. The accelerating explosion of satanism worldwide is a phenomenon peculiar to our time making the thought of the world worshiping Satan far more plausible than in past generations.

At the same time that the world is being set up to worship the Antichrist, so is the professing Christian church. Paul's warnings concerning apostasy, or a turning away from the faith in the last days, are many. One of the specifics he mentions seems unbelievable: "The Spirit speaketh expressly that in the latter times some shall depart from the faith [apostatize], giving heed to seducing spirits and doctrines of devils" (1 Timothy 4:1). Such a prophecy is shocking: that a characteristic of the last days will be trafficking with evil spirits by those who call or have called themselves Christians! Yet our generation is experiencing this to a degree never before known in history.

There have always been attempts to contact the spirit world through seances, Ouija boards, and other divination devices. Very few participants were involved, however, and they rarely admitted the practice, which was generally conducted in semidarkness and

> The world of our day is unquestionably being prepared for the one who "as God sitteth in the temple of God, showing himself that he is God."
> —2 Thessalonians 2:4

was always looked at askance by the average person. But today spiritism is practiced by scores of millions of people around the world, although under a variety of new forms and called by different names that make it widely acceptable.

In the church, too, there is a departure from the faith but in the name of faith. Seducing spirits are being contacted, but here they don't pose as "deeper levels of the psyche" or as "ascended masters" but as Christ Himself. The practice of visualizing "Jesus" is being used in "inner healing" and in order to enhance one's prayer life or to gain a deeper insight into what Jesus taught.

The visualized "Jesus" literally moves on its own and speaks in its own voice. Contact has been made with a demonic spirit, not with Jesus, who does not appear in response to visualization. This powerful occult technique is exactly how witchdoctors conjure up their spirit guides—and now it is in the church. The explosion of this phenomenon worldwide to become rampant even in the church is unique to our generation and provides further evidence that we could be in the *last* of the last days.

Paul was given remarkable insights which are so uniquely applicable to our modern world that they could not possibly have come to him by any means except divine inspiration. He warned: "...in the last days perilous times shall come. For men shall be lovers of their own selves" (2 Timothy 3:1,2). Mankind has always been self-centered, selfish, and narcissistic. Our generation, however, is the first one in history that is being *taught* to love self. It is now widely accepted that we naturally dislike ourselves and must *learn* to love ourselves before we can love God or other people. The first commandment has become "Thou shalt love thyself," relegating "Thou shalt love the Lord thy God" to second place.

Christ would never have said "Do unto others as you would have them do unto you" if we all disliked ourselves. His command to "love your neighbor as yourself" obviously assumes that we already love ourselves and is not intended to encourage but to *correct* self-love. It urges us to give to our neighbors some of the loving care we naturally lavish upon ourselves. Yet some evangelical churches hold seminars to teach members how to love themselves. It is like pouring gasoline on a fire already out of control. And once again the prophesied phenomenon has appeared for the first time in our present generation.

John also saw in his vision that not only the Dragon (Satan) would be worshiped, but that the Antichrist himself would be worshiped as God. Past generations would have thought it ridiculous to imagine that anyone, much less the entire world, would worship a man as *God*. In the last 40 years, however, the "god-men" from the East such as Bhagwan Shri

Rajneesh, Baba Muktananda, Maharaji, and many others have come to the West and have been literally worshiped as God by thousands of their followers. While only a small minority of mankind currently follow the gurus, nevertheless worshiping a man as God has for the first time in history become commonplace in the Western world. Actors, actresses, sports heroes, and political leaders are among those now worshiping gurus.

The world of our day is unquestionably being prepared for the one who "as God sitteth in the temple of God, showing himself that he is God" (2 Thessalonians 2:4). This prophecy will have its primary fulfillment when the Antichrist sits in the Jewish temple yet to be rebuilt in Jerusalem. There is, however, a secondary application. The body of a believer becomes the "temple" of God through the indwelling of the Holy Spirit ("ye are the temple of God, and...the Spirit of God dwelleth in you"—1 Corinthians 3:16; see also 6:19)—and so it should be with all mankind. Instead, the religion of the Antichrist exalts *self* as "God" within the human "temple."

Today, for the first time in history, not only a few Yogis and gurus but increasing millions of ordinary people worldwide are mystically looking deep within themselves. There, in what ought to be the temple of the true God, they seek to discover that their alleged "higher self" is "God." The practice of TM, Eastern meditation, and other forms of yoga is widespread. The goal is "self-realization," to realize that one is "God." It is the very same lie with which the serpent deceived Eve. Obviously the deification of self plays an important part in preparing the world to worship the Antichrist, giving us yet another indication that our generation could be living in the *last* of the last days.

Jesus warned that the major sign heralding the nearness of His return would be religious deception: "Take heed that no man deceive you." He went on to explain the elements of that last-days' deception: "Many false prophets shall rise, and shall deceive many...For there shall arise false Christs and false prophets, and shall show great signs and wonders, insomuch that, if it were possible, they shall deceive the very elect" (Matthew 24:4,11,24).

A secular analyst writing even 50 years ago would not have predicted the worldwide religious revival that Christ prophesied. Instead, he would have suggested that our day would be characterized by skepticism and atheism, and that science would have advanced so far that there would be little place for religion in the world. No educated person would give credence to "spiritual values," but materialism would have taken over completely.

How wrong such an analyst would have been! In contrast, how right Christ was in saying that *many* false prophets and false messiahs would arise and deceive *many*. The implication was clear: A revival of religion would sweep the world in the last days. It would not, however, represent the truth; instead, multitudes would be deceived by false prophets and false messiahs. The accuracy of this remarkable 2000-year-old prophecy cannot be denied.

The situation in the church today is reminiscent of the last days of Israel's kingdom. Instead of heeding God's Word, God's people consulted spirit mediums (Isaiah 8:19). Israel had sunk into the mire of occultism, astrology, and idolatry (Jeremiah 19:4,5,13; 32:29). Immorality was rampant even among the priests (Ezekiel 16:15-59; Hosea 6:9). God's righteous judgment was about to fall, as it is upon today's church and world. Nebuchadnezzar's army would be the instrument, and the seventy-year Babylonian captivity for God's chosen people would begin.

Israel desperately needed rescue from a merciless, invincible invading army, but deliverance could only come through repentance and submission to her Lord. God had patiently sent prophet after prophet to indict Israel with her rebellion, idolatry, wickedness, and occult practices and to plead with her to repent, but she would not. She needed to face the truth, but turned instead to the numerous false prophets who lulled her to sleep with their soothing lies.

Their "positive" message was far more appealing than the "negative" pronouncements of those who spoke for God. In the face of misleading assurances that all was well, Isaiah gave solemn notice: "There is no peace, saith my God, to the wicked" (57:21).

Earnestly Jeremiah warned of God's impending judgment against the positive-thinking false prophets who promised Israel "Peace, peace, when there is no peace" (6:14; 8:11). Calling such deceitful assurances "vain vision" and "flattering divination" (12:24), Ezekiel declared:

> Therefore thus saith the Lord: Because ye have spoken vanity and seen lies...I am against you... mine hand shall be upon the prophets that see vanity and that divine lies....
> Because...they have seduced my people, saying, Peace; and there was no peace...(13:8-10).

We live in a similar twilight of history. This time it is settling over the entire world. Once again those who warn of God's soon-coming judgment are accused of being negative. The cure-all magic of a Positive Mental Attitude (PMA) is widely taught in the secular world of business, psychology, education, medicine—and also in the church.

Many Christians now assume that our thoughts and words, not God, control our destiny—that we are little gods under Him capable of creating our own world. Such a philosophy seems at obvious odds with Christ's prayer in the Garden of Gethsemane:

> Father, all things are possible unto thee; take away this cup [of the cross] from me; nevertheless not what I will, but what thou wilt (Mark 14:36).

Presumably, if Christ had only understood and practiced the "principles of success" that are now being taught in the church, the New Testament would have had a different story to tell. Had He only taken a Dale Carnegie course in "How to

> Heaven is our real home and that is where our hearts are—with Him. The world has lost its appeal, sin has lost its power, and Satan must relinquish his claim upon those who belong to Christ. We have been set free!

Win Friends and Influence People," He could have won the rabbis and Romans over to His side and wouldn't have been crucified. Instead of making enemies by His negative pronouncements, His goals could all have been worked out peacefully by the principles of Positive Thinking and ecumenical cooperation.

While being soothingly assured by today's "prophets" that we are in the "greatest revival ever," the church is sinking deeper into the last-days apostasy foretold by Christ and His apostles. More than 30 years ago A.W. Tozer preached that, rather than "revival," the church desperately needed *reformation*.

Meanwhile, the prospects of a humanistic world peace grow ever brighter. Man seems on the verge of solving his problems without God. "Peace and safety" is the swelling cry. It is the greatest of delusions, the deceptive calm before the storm. Mankind is about to reap the full wrath of God for its rejection of His Son, who Himself is poised to return in vengeance. Surely the signs which herald the Second Coming are already casting their shadows to signal that our generation is living in the *last* of the last days.

When each of the events we have so far considered stands alone, its value as a "last-days sign" may not seem too impressive. But when we see the convergence of all these events within the same time frame the pieces of the puzzle begin to fit together.

For those who truly belong to Christ, though they mourn for the delusion and disaster they see coming upon the world, there is the joy and excitement of knowing that it cannot be long until they will hear that shout from Christ Himself calling them to meet Him in the air.

Christ could come at any moment to take us to His Father's house, where we will be united with Him eternally. Seven years later, when He appears and "every eye shall see Him" and Israel will recognize Him, we will be at His side in glorified bodies to rule and reign with Him—"and so shall we ever be with the Lord!" That is the Christian's hope. Heaven is our real home and that is where our hearts are— with Him. The world has lost its appeal, sin has lost its power, and Satan must relinquish his claim upon those who belong to Christ. We have been set free!

What motivation that realization gives both for holy living and for declaring with clarity God's message to mankind! And what is that message? The standard "evangelistic" approach has long been to promise healing and joy and blessing for those who come to Christ, but a world that imagines it is in the process of achieving peace and prosperity has little motivation for heeding such a gospel.

The message that is needed is one of conviction of sin and the fear of God. Until men and women realize that they have violated God's laws and that this world is ripening to reap His wrath, they will not see their need for the forgiveness which Christ bought with His blood. That message will be increasingly difficult to deliver in the days ahead, but it is the only one that will prevent "converts" from coming to Christ for the wrong reasons and thereby being set up to follow the Antichrist when he appears. It is both awesome and thrilling to realize that our responsibility and privilege is to rescue as many as possible from the wrath to come.

Part V

The Hope
of Heaven

26

The Reality of Heaven
for the Believer

*In my Father's house are many mansions: if it
were not so, I would have told you. I go to prepare
a place for you. And if I go and prepare a place for
you, I will come again, and receive you unto
myself; that where I am, there ye may be also.*
—JOHN 14:2,3

The Bible begins with God creating the universe and it ends with Him destroying it entirely and creating afresh a "new heaven and a new earth" (Revelation 21:1). From beginning to end, history is the eternal God fulfilling His immutable purpose. Once we get a clear view of the cosmic proportions of God's plan, we lose any delusions as to our own greatness and are delivered from all mistaken notions that we can somehow fulfill human destiny by our own efforts.

Of course that very delusion fuels the humanist's cosmic aspirations. As part of SETI (Search for Extraterrestrial Intelligence), President Carter, a professing Christian, cast this message into the cosmos aboard the *Voyager* spacecraft. It was addressed to any spacefaring civilization that might chance to intercept *Voyager*:

> This is a present from a small distant world...
> attempting to survive our time so we may live into
> yours. We hope someday...to join a community of
> galactic civilizations. This [is] our hope and our
> determination...in a vast and awesome universe.
> —Jimmy Carter, President of the United States
> The White House, June 16, 1977

Far from hoping to join a community of galactic civilizations, the Christian looks forward to the destruction of the present cosmos and the creation by God of a new universe that will be inhabited by a new race of twice-born children of God, who have received Jesus Christ as Savior and Lord and have been made new creations in Him. Once that tremendous fact grips one's heart it becomes clear why salvation must be by grace alone; it is nothing that we deserve or could accomplish, but it must be entirely God doing for us what we could never do for ourselves.

A new heaven and a new earth inhabited by a new race descended from a new Adam, Jesus Christ Himself! That is God's purpose and it is staggering to contemplate. From this perspective, it is ludicrous to imagine that the church, by organizing conservative voters or even by preaching the gospel, is going to establish God's kingdom. The true and eternal kingdom of God involves not just this small planet but all creation, including the purging by the blood of Jesus and the remaking of heaven itself.

> Throughout Scripture we are counseled to live at all times with the understanding that life on this earth is very brief and that it is followed by an eternal existence.

Nothing could be better established from Scripture and logic than the glorious fact that the ultimate fulfillment of God's purpose is something that only He can accomplish. Obviously we can only be part of that plan as we allow Him to have His way in and through us.

This realization puts us on our faces before God in wonder and worship, and causes us to yield ourselves wholeheartedly to His will. Unfortunately, that awesome sense of the greatness of God and the cosmic and eternal proportions of the work that He is doing seems largely absent from Christianity today. Could this be why so many carry the self-imposed burdens of the many "programs" they are trying to put into effect in order to "live victorious lives" or to "advance the cause of Christ"? When we see that the task is totally beyond our capabilities, then we cease from our striving and begin to allow Him to work in and through us by His mighty power.

Many object to this heavenly/eternal perspective as "pie-in-the-sky in the sweet by-and-by" talk. There are warnings about being so "heavenly minded" that one is of "no earthly good." We must be practical, so the argument goes, meeting first of all the earthly needs of ourselves and of others and doing our best to make this world a better place for everyone.

Yet Christ Himself continually turned the focus of His followers from earth to heaven. Throughout Scripture we are counseled to live at all times with the understanding that life on this earth is very brief and that it is followed by an eternal existence of either indescribable bliss in God's presence or unbearable agony in separation from Him. Peter declares that the knowledge that "the heavens shall pass away with a great noise...[and] the earth also and the works that are therein shall be burned up" (2 Peter 3:10) causes us to live godly lives. And John adds that the hope of being transformed into His likeness when He shall appear causes us to purify ourselves (1 John 3:2,3).

Of course, the greatest motivation is the love that is born in our hearts as we realize that the Creator of the universe loves each of us so much that He became a man to die in our place. This love has captured our affection so that we gladly declare that we are His and His alone for eternity. Accepting the death of Jesus Christ as our own death, we have given up life as we would have lived it so that He can live His resurrection life through us. The eternal kingdom has already begun in every heart where the King reigns! Moreover, as His bride, we long to be united in that heavenly marriage with Christ our Bridegroom and to honeymoon with Him forever in His Father's house! Forever we will worship and praise the One who has made all things new!

Many would have us believe that self-love is *the* answer to the world's ills. Both Christian leaders and the unsaved are teaching and preaching this lie. In fact, it is self-love that has wrought the ills of the world: greed, lust, and envy. What we actually need is a passionate love for God and His Word, turning us from earthly ambitions to heavenly hope.

Peace cannot be achieved personally until the Prince of Peace, Jesus Christ, reigns in our hearts. And peace on this earth will not be seen until the King of kings comes to reign. But startlingly enough, even His presence will not turn men from their determination to rule their own kingdom. Not even a kingdom ruled by Christ on this earth is our hope, but heaven itself; and in the new heavens and new earth God's will is finally done "on earth as it is in heaven" because heaven and earth have become one.

While the millennium is commonly referred to as the Kingdom of God for which Jesus taught His disciples to pray ("Thy kingdom come..."), that cannot be true for several obvious reasons. Foremost of all, the millennium ends after 1000 years. But the Word of God distinctly tells us that God's kingdom "is an everlasting kingdom" (Psalm 145:13). Even Babylon's King Nebuchadnezzar knew that "his [God's] kingdom is an everlasting kingdom..." (Daniel 4:3).

Daniel reiterates that fact (7:14), as does Isaiah in his prophecy of the Messiah who will rule restored Israel: "For unto us a child is born, unto us a son is given: and the government shall be upon his shoulders. And his name shall be called Wonderful, Counselor, the mighty God, the everlasting Father..."(9:6). The next verse, often overlooked, is conclusive, "and in the increase of his government and peace there shall be no end." *No end!*

Yet the millennium ends, and with earth's final war. At that time Jesus himself has been reigning on David's throne for 1000 years during which Satan has been confined to "the bottomless pit" so that he could "deceive the nations no more" (Revelation 20:1-3). Christ has established peace on earth and has enforced it with a rod of iron (Psalm 2). The lion lies down with the lamb and eats straw like an ox (Isaiah 65:25). Yet as soon as Satan is released, mankind "the number of whom is as the sand of the sea" follow him in battle against Christ in Jerusalem (Revelation 20:7-9). That war alone disqualifies the millennium from being God's kingdom of endless peace.

There are other disqualifications. Jesus told Nicodemus that no one can even see, much less enter into, the Kingdom of God without being born again of the Holy Spirit (John 3:1-16). Yet multitudes living in the millennial kingdom will not have been born again, providing another reason why it is not the Kingdom of God. Paul declared, "Flesh and blood cannot inherit the kingdom of God" (1 Corinthians 15:50). But there will be millions of "flesh-and-blood" people living in the millennium—a further reason why it is not the Kingdom of God.

Then what is the millennium? Quite clearly, it is God's final proof of the incorrigible evil of the human heart. Even Christ, having turned earth into a paradise rivaling the Garden of Eden, ruling with a rod of iron and the redeemed in glorified bodies reigning with Him cannot change the human heart or make men willingly obey Him. There is no way to reform the present human race. It must be put to death in Christ and created anew through faith in Him. The kingdom begins in individual hearts when Christ the King is received to reign within.

When finally the Kingdom of God is realized it will be in a completely new universe to replace the present one which will have been destroyed by one great conflagration (2 Peter 3:10-13). That new creation will be inhabited only by sinless angels and men and women who themselves have been made new creations through faith in Christ. Then heaven and earth will be one with God's will truly done on earth as it is in heaven. This is the bright future true believers look forward to for all eternity.

Meanwhile, in this present world of evil and tribulation, it is not unusual for a believer to feel discouraged and even depressed by his or her own failure. At such times it seems impossible to believe that God could ever be pleased with us or that He would really accept us into heaven. We find it so very difficult to rest in His grace and love when we realize that we are absolutely unworthy of heaven. Yet our greatest joy comes from the wonder, amazement, and gratitude that He would take such wretched, unworthy sinners and grant us the joy of heaven!

We will never be worthy of heaven or of His love. That sense of self-worth which so many Christian leaders, deceived by Christian psychology, are attempting to foster among the redeemed, would ruin heaven by turning some of the attention and glory from God and the Lamb to ourselves. We will always be creatures and He the Creator; we will always be sinners saved by grace and bought with His blood, and He will ever be our glorious Savior. Because His infinite love for us has filled us with love for Him, our passion for eternity will ever be to see Him exalted and praised and to love Him with all the capacity He supplies. His eternal joy will be to bless us with Himself. Such will be the wonder and ecstasy of heaven.

God desires to have us in His presence even more than we could ever desire to be there. He loves us with a love that will never let us go. And because He has captured our affection, we will be eternally bound by love to Him—a love that not only flows to us from God, but which our redeemed hearts will return to Him with a purity and heavenly joy that will be to His eternal glory.

The signs that His return is near are in the world today as never before. The sleeping church may soon be shaken with that cry of which Christ spoke in parable:

> While the bridegroom tarried, they all slumbered and slept. And at midnight there was a cry made, "Behold the bridegroom cometh; go ye out to meet him" (Matthew 25:5,6).

27

The Believer's Hope

*When Christ, who is our life, shall appear, then
shall ye also appear with him in glory.*
—COLOSSIANS 3:4

One cannot read the New Testament without seeing its
heavenly orientation. Heaven was continually on the heart of
our Lord and it was the context for everything that He taught
His disciples. He made it clear that He was calling them to
turn their attention and affection and interest from this
world to heaven, from what had been their earthly home and
hope to His "Father's house" from whence He had come and
to which He would soon take them. He tried to wean them
away from their natural earthly mindedness to heavenly
mindedness by contrasting the superiority and eternality of
heaven with the empty and temporal nature of all this world
has to offer.

Christ had said that His true disciples were "in the
world" but "not of the world" because He had chosen them
"out of the world" (John 17:6,11,14-18). There can be no
doubt that the hope of the early Christians was not in the
future of certain persecution which they faced on this earth,
but in leaving earth for heaven to be forever with their Lord.

They knew that they were "partakers of the heavenly calling" (Hebrews 3:1). Their only reliable and worthwhile hope was "laid up for [them] in heaven" (Colossians 1:5). Typical of the way in which our Lord continually sought to turn His disciples from this earth to heaven is the following exhortation:

> Lay not up for yourselves treasures upon earth, where moth and rust doth corrupt, and where thieves break through and steal, but lay up for yourselves treasures in heaven, where neither moth nor rust doth corrupt, and where thieves do not break through nor steal, for where your treasure is, there will your heart be also (Matthew 6:19,20).

In sharp contrast to such commands from Christ and the heavenly orientation of the early church, there is a large and growing number of Christians today for whom long-range earthly ambitions have all but obscured the traditional hope of heaven—ambitions which they believe to be not carnal but biblical and very spiritual. They have become convinced that the Great Commission calls for a reconstruction of society that will result in a "Christianized" world. Since they believe that this reconstruction could take a long time, even thousands of years, it makes no sense not to lay up treasure upon this earth.

Our hope, our ambition, our desire, our passion, and our dreams for the future are all to involve our eternal home in heaven.

Unfortunately, the "take-over-the-world-for-Christ" advocates find themselves in direct conflict with the Lord's specific commands. Of course, they could argue that none of us follows the above admonition to the letter. Even those who believe in Christ's imminent return and expect to leave it all behind at any moment nevertheless have savings accounts, buy homes, and build churches and Christian schools.

There is, however, a great difference in attitude and incentive between those who are motivated to live for Christ and eternity by the realization that statistically—for a very small percentage of the population—death could come prematurely and unexpectedly and those who sincerely believe that Christ could take all Christians home at any moment. The latter hold the things of this earth far more loosely.

Paul wrote: "If (since) ye then be risen with Christ, seek those things which are above, where Christ sitteth on the right hand of God. Set your affection on things above, not on things on the earth" (Colossians 3:1,2). Our hope, our ambition, our desire, our passion, and our dreams for the future are all to involve our eternal home in heaven and not what we can achieve or accumulate on this earth. To call that impractical is to deny the inspiration of Scripture. We are in this world but not of it, using but not abusing it, considering everything in this life of transitory worth.

This does not mean that we have no concern for the poor or that we do not actively seek to improve the moral and social climate of our world. Yet everything we do to benefit others on this earth must be done not for its social value alone but for the sake of Christ and for the glory of God. Furthermore, rescuing souls for heaven must always take precedence over providing people with earth benefits. The old saying that a person can be "so heavenly minded as to be no earthly good" is popular but false. Clearly no one could be more heavenly minded than Christ, nor could anyone be of more earthly good than He. His life is our model in keeping the proper balance.

It is because there is so little appreciation of what the New Testament teaches, that heaven (and hell as well) seem so nebulous and of such doubtful importance alongside the great plans we have for "changing the world for Christ." Could this also be why so much that is presented as Christianity today is simply a sanctification of worldly desires in the name of Jesus? The same selfish ambitions and longings which motivate the world, the same fleshly goals, and the same kind of success are offered as enticements to get people to "come to Jesus"—a "Jesus" who never rebukes sin but only heals, prospers, and "positively reinforces" one's self-esteem.

Many Christians imagine that victory in Christ is to become the epitome of what the world desires in wealth and success and fame and to do it all better than the ungodly because Christians have Jesus on their side. Such is the misguided promise of positive confession. Though such a false hope may seemingly be supported by an isolated verse here or there taken out of context, it is the very antithesis of the consistent message of the New Testament.

Christ did make promises, of course, for this earthly existence. He told His disciples that those who would leave father or mother or lands or houses for His sake would receive a hundredfold in this life. He was not granting *ownership* of these benefits, however, as is suggested by positive confession advocates, who promise that God will return $100,000 for every $1,000 given to their ministries. Christ offered something more wonderful than the hundredfold accumulation of great properties, luxury autos, and abundant goods. He promised that we would be taken into the homes and share the provisions of many others who know and love Him and who would love us, too, as brothers and sisters in the same heavenly and eternal family of God.

> The Christian's hope is the return of Christ to take him to heaven, to be glorified with Christ in His kingdom, and to share His triumphant reign over this earth.

At the same time, however, Christ reminds us that inevitably these blessings come wrapped in "persecutions" (Mark 10:30) as part of the package—persecutions that we are to experience as long as we remain upon earth. Unless, of course, we deny our Lord or compromise our faith. Then and only then can we expect to be popular with the world.

The Bible makes it abundantly clear that those who would be honored in this world rob themselves of heaven's eternal rewards. Insight into what it means to "let this mind be in you, which was also in Christ Jesus" (Philippians 2:5) is found in these words from our Lord:

> I receive not honor from men. How can ye believe [be men and women of faith], which receive honor one of another, and seek not the honor that cometh from God only? (John 5:41,44).

The Christian's hope is the return of Christ to take him to heaven, to be glorified with Christ in His kingdom, and to share His triumphant reign over this earth. "And when the chief shepherd shall appear," wrote Peter, "ye shall receive a crown of glory that fadeth not away" (1 Peter 5:4). Referring to the same event, Paul wrote: "When Christ, who is our life, shall appear, then shall ye also appear with him in glory" (Colossians 3:4).

Paul cultivated among all of the believers in his day the eager expectancy that this appearing would take place very soon. In so doing he attempted, like His Lord, to wean them from this earth to live as those who were already citizens of heaven. To the Philippians he wrote: "For our conversation [citizenship] is in heaven, from whence also we look for the Savior, the Lord Jesus Christ..." (Philippians 3:20). And to Titus: "Looking for that blessed hope, and the glorious appearing of the great God and our Savior Jesus Christ" (Titus 2:13).

There are those who argue that it is foolish to think of Christ returning today, since the apostles vainly expected that great event in their time. On the contrary, they did not—yet they urged the Christians of their day to remain expectant. The apostle Paul unquestionably knew that this longed-for event would not occur during his own lifetime, which would be cut short by Roman execution. He told Timothy, "The time of my departure [by death] is at hand" (2 Timothy 11:6). And he told the Ephesian elders, "after my departing [in death] shall grievous wolves enter in among you..." (Acts 20:29).

Peter also had the same conviction, as his writings prove. He, too, spoke of his impending death. "Knowing that shortly I must put off this my tabernacle [of flesh and blood]...I will endeavor [through his written epistles] that ye may be able after my decease to have these things always in remembrance" (2 Peter 1:14,15).

The apostles knew that they were "appointed to death...a spectacle unto the world" (1 Corinthians 4:9). Only the apostle John, of whom the Lord had said, "If I will that he tarry till I come..." (John 21:22), was the lone exception among them. He was spared martyrdom, yet died without seeing that promised coming.

This same apostle John tells us that the earnest expectation of Christ's imminent appearing, and our deliverance from sin and death by transformation into glorious bodies like His, will inevitably have a powerful and purifying effect in every area of our lives. He wrote:

> Beloved, now are we the sons of God, and it doth not yet appear what we shall be; but we know that, when he shall appear, we shall be like him, for we shall see him as he is.
> And every man that hath this hope in him purifieth himself, even as he is pure (1 John 3:2,3).

Paul declared that when Christ returned, as He had promised, He would resurrect the dead and catch away all living Christians together with them to meet Him in the air (1 Thessalonians 4:13-18). No adventure could be more rapturous, so the word "rapture"—which in English means a sudden and ecstatic catching away—was adopted to describe this unprecedented event. Moreover, the word "rapture," while not found in English translations of the Bible, is the Latin word for "caught up" (1 Thessalonians 4:17) used in the Latin Vulgate translation, and is therefore quite biblical.

With respect to Christ's return, we are repeatedly urged to be in an attitude of *watching and waiting*:

> Let your loins be girded about, and your lights burning; and ye yourselves like unto men that wait for their lord...Be ye therefore ready also: for the Son of man cometh at an hour when ye think not (Luke 12:35-40)

We do well to consider why this continual expectancy of His imminent return, which is unquestionably commanded by Christ, should have such a special purifying effect. Oddly enough, it seems quite apparent that its value for us, and the importance the Bible obviously attaches to it, do not depend upon whether the Lord's return actually occurs in our lifetime or not. It is the eager *expectancy* that counts and which is not only a major purifying factor, as John says, but must also be a barometer of our spiritual life.

While there are many indications that the Lord's return may very well be imminent for *us*, we now know in retrospect that it was *not* imminent for all those generations of Christians who came before us. If the sole value of their "expectancy" lay in its being satisfied by the Lord's actual return during their lifetime, then the fact that Christ has not yet returned would mean that they waited and watched in vain. Yet the Lord urged this "expectant" attitude upon His first disciples, knowing full well that they and millions of Christians would be taken to heaven in death before He returned. Therefore, there must be something important, something integral to a good Christian life, about the mere *attitude* of expecting at any moment Christ's return and our transformation into His likeness. Why?

There can be no doubt that a conviction that we could be caught up into heaven at any moment would impart an added seriousness to our lives. The transient nature of our earthly tenure should cause us to make every moment count for eternity. In this regard, the expectancy of Christ's imminent return should weaken our tendency to identify ourselves too closely with a world which does not hold our ultimate destiny. It should also help to remind us of our true citizenship in a world to come which is based upon eternal rather than earthly values. This attitude certainly ought to characterize a Christian life, and a lively sense of the possibility of Christ's imminent return is more than justified if it has this wholesome effect.

Recognizing that one could momentarily be taken to heaven in the rapture also presents a profoundly sobering challenge to examine the reality of one's faith (2 Corinthians 13:5). But doesn't the possibility of imminent death have the same effect? There are several reasons why it does not. The expectancy of being caught up at any moment into the presence of our Lord in the rapture has some definite advantages over a similar expectancy through the possibility of sudden death.

First of all, if we are in a right relationship with Christ, we can genuinely look forward to the rapture. Yet no one (not even Christ in the Garden) looks forward to death. The joyful prospect of the rapture will attract our thoughts, while the distasteful prospect of death is something we may try to forget, thus making it less effective in our daily lives.

Moreover, while the rapture is similar to death in that both serve to end our earthly life, the rapture does something else as well: It signals the climax of history and opens the curtain upon earth's final drama. It thus ends, in a way that death does not, all human stake in continuing earthly developments, such as the lives of one's children left behind, the growth or dispersion of one's accumulated fortune, the protection of one's personal reputation, the success of whatever earthly causes one has espoused, and all other seemingly legitimate interests which bind us to this present world. The rapture strips us of earthly hope and purifies our hearts in a way that death does not.

Furthermore, the incentive provided by death is also weakened by the fact that we generally have at least some control over its relative imminence. Certainly we are radically contingent beings, and our lives may be snuffed out at any time. But this is not the way people usually die. The cancer victim might have refrained from smoking, or added more fiber to his diet, or sought treatment earlier. The guilty auto accident victim could have driven within the speed limit or taken a taxi when he had too much to drink.

Though death can come suddenly and without warning (we are not complete masters of our own fate), it is nevertheless true that we make decisions daily that increase or decrease the chances of our dying tomorrow, next month, or in ten years. This not-altogether-illusory sense of control over the time of our demise reduces the incentive for godliness by making us feel that we can afford to postpone a closer relationship with God until next week, next month, or next year. We expect to have at least some warning when death is coming close and imagine that there will be time to let go of the earthly and live fully for the heavenly.

In contrast, we have absolutely no control over the timing of the rapture. It will just happen "out of the blue"— and for many of us, as Christ warned, when we least expect Him (Matthew 24:44). Belief in the imminent return of Christ, then, does not allow us to postpone anything or substitute anything for that blessed hope, and thus it has a most powerful purifying effect upon those who truly have their hearts fixed on the glorious hope of an imminent rapture.

28

The Bride
of Christ

*I have espoused you to one husband, that I may
present you as a chaste virgin to Christ.*
—1 CORINTHIANS 11:2

If we take the Bible seriously, then we will long for our
Lord to catch us away from this earth into His eternal presence. Among the many reasons why we ought to be eagerly
looking for the rapture, the most compelling is neither theological nor eschatological, but is our love for Christ. If the
church is indeed His bride, then surely we ought to be
eagerly anticipating His return to take us to His Father's
house for our marriage to Him. Here we have the most basic
and yet most neglected
aspect of heaven—that it is
to be the scene of a great
wedding that our Savior has
long anticipated. How can
His bride not share that
joyful hope?

> The church is likened in
> Scripture to the bride of Christ
> and finally is called His "wife."

There can be little doubt that the church is likened in
Scripture to the bride of Christ and finally is called His

"wife." In expressing his concern that the Corinthian believers not be deceived by Satan, Paul said, "I have espoused you to one husband, that I may present you as a chaste virgin to Christ" (2 Corinthians 11:2). Israel had already been called God's wife in the Old Testament, an adulterous wife to whom He will yet be reconciled. Thus she could scarcely be the virgin referred to above. To the Ephesians, Paul used the relationship between Christ and the church to express how husbands and wives were to relate in love to each other:

> For the husband is the head of the wife, even as Christ is the head of the church...Therefore as the church is subject unto Christ, so let the wives be to their own husbands in every thing. Husbands, love your wives, even as Christ also loved the church, and gave himself for it...For this cause shall a man leave his father and mother, and shall be joined unto his wife, and they two shall be one flesh. This is a great mystery; but I speak concerning Christ and the church (Ephesians 5:22-33).

In picturing His Second Coming, Christ told a number of parables involving weddings. Much of the terminology He used was right out of Jewish marriage traditions known to His listeners. In *A Christian Love Story*, Zola Levitt relates that tradition and explains how beautifully it fits the promises that Jesus gave His disciples. Presenting the results of his research of rabbinical sources, Levitt writes:

> When that matter (of the marriage contract and price to be paid for the bride) was settled the groom would depart. He would make a little speech to his (espoused) bride, saying, "I go to prepare a place for you," and he would return to his father's house. Back at his father's house, he would build her a bridal chamber, a little mansion, in which they would have their future honeymoon... remain(ing) inside for seven days...At the end of the week, the bride and groom would make their long-awaited appearance...(and) there would be

a...marriage supper, which we might refer to as the wedding reception...This construction project would take the better part of a year...and the father of the groom would be the judge of when it was finished...The bride, for her part, was obliged to do a lot of waiting... (and) she had to have an oil lamp ready in case he came late at night...she had to be ready to travel at a moment's notice... (The groom) and his young men would set out in the night, making every attempt to completely surprise the bride...The church is called "the bride of Christ" in the New Testament for good reason.

One can readily see that Christ expected His disciples to understand what He said in reference to such a tradition. His statement, "In my Father's house are many mansions...I go to prepare a place for you...and will come again to receive you unto myself," clearly depicted Him as the groom and those who believed on Him as His espoused bride. His statement, "But of that day and that hour knoweth no man... neither the Son, but the Father" (Mark 13:32) was not a denial of His deity and omniscience. It pointed again to the wedding tradition with which His listeners were familiar. The bridegroom couldn't just throw a lean-to together and rush off and claim his bride. It was up to the father to decide when the honeymoon cottage was suitable; then he would tell the groom that he could bring his bride there.

> It was up to the father to decide when the honeymoon cottage was suitable; then he would tell the groom that he could bring his bride there.

The Lord, as we have seen, presented the gospel as involving not so much a choice between heaven and hell but between heaven and this earth. And those who opt for this earth, which is slated for destruction, end up in hell: "For what is a man profited, if he shall gain the whole world and lose his own soul? Or what shall a man give in exchange for his soul?" (Matthew 16:26). The desires and ambitions of this life all too often lure us away from the eternal home Christ offers. We cannot live both for this world and the next. What we do in this world must primarily have heaven in view or it could cost us heaven.

In all honesty, however, the longing to be raptured home to heaven imminently does not come easily. There should be a great conflict in the heart of every true Christian. On the one hand there ought to be a genuine longing for Christ to return so that we can see Him at last, fall at His feet, and enjoy the bliss of His presence forevermore. On the other hand, however, there ought to be a passion to win the lost to Christ before it is too late—and that would cause us to want more time in which to fulfill the Great Commission. He, in fact, has delayed His coming for that very reason (2 Peter 3:9). For many people today, however, there is no conflict at all because they no longer believe that departing to be with Christ at any moment in the rapture is even possible, much less something to be desired.

How could we genuinely long for His imminent return if we still had loved ones who were not believers and who would therefore be left behind to be separated from God and from us forever? Christ confronted those who wanted to be His disciples with this very dilemma. "He that loveth father or mother more than me is not worthy of me," He told them. "And he that loveth son or daughter more than me is not worthy of me" (Matthew 10:37). A difficult choice, perhaps, but once made there must be no regrets. In fact, He said we must hate our own lives and abandon everything—nothing must stand in the way of our devotion to Him. Is that too much for the Lord of glory, who gave Himself for us, to ask?

One of the most beautiful Old Testament pictures of the church as the bride of Christ is found in Genesis 24. Abraham's servant, a type of the Holy Spirit, had claimed Rebekah as Isaac's bride. As it is with us, however, she had to choose for herself between the husband waiting for her in a far country and the family she would have to leave in order to join him. "Wilt thou go with this man?" her family asked her. And she said, "I will go."

Such is the choice that confronts us. It is a choice that countless earthly brides have made and not regretted. No less is demanded by our Lord of His heavenly bride.

In contrast to the attitude of the early church, however, heaven has become for many in today's church that place that everyone wants to go to—but not yet. Surely the Bridegroom must grieve over a bride that is so reluctant to join Him in that great heavenly marriage.

Is it not time that the bride of Christ, laying all else aside, became excited about the prospect of seeing and being with her Bridegroom forever? Oh, that a great cry would arise from the church: "We love You, Lord Jesus! Please come and take us home! The Spirit and the bride say, Come! Come, Lord Jesus, come!"

29

God Has Said, "I Love You!"

I have loved thee with an everlasting love: there-
fore with lovingkindness I have drawn thee.
—JEREMIAH 31:3

For God so loved the world, that he gave his only
begotten Son, that whosoever believeth in him
should not perish, but have everlasting life.
—JOHN 3:16

God has given mankind marvelous abilities. Think of the great scientists and philosophers who have probed the mysteries of life; and the poets, novelists, and musicians who have expressed the depth of human experience in compelling ways. Nor is it any less marvelous that our imagination can take ideas presented merely in words and can transform them into deep emotions of excitement, surprise, grief, and joy.

It has been suggested that the unique ability to form conceptual ideas and to express them in speech separates

> We are made in the image of God, who, speaking of Himself, has said "God is love."

mankind from all lower creatures by a chasm that no evolutionary process could ever span. While that is true, there is another capacity which separates man even further from animals. Paul explained it thus: "Though I speak with the tongues of men and of angels, and have not [love], I am become as sounding brass, or a tinkling cymbal" (1 Corinthians 13:1). To put it in a contemporary context, without love man is a robot, a computer programmed to meaningless reactions. In a word, it is *love* that makes a human being.

Without love, Paul reminds us, we are nothing. That "nothing" doesn't mean that we don't exist, but that we are not what we were intended to be by our Creator. We are not fully human without love, no matter how much knowledge we have or how clever we are. It should be clear why this is the case. We are made in the image of God, who, speaking of Himself, has said "God is love." Thus the very essence of the Creator who made man in His image must be the essence of man the creature. And it is in the perversion of that essence that we have ample proof that something went horribly wrong.

We do not need to know Greek and the difference between the types of love (for which Greek has separate words) to realize that the love which Paul goes on to describe in 1 Corinthians 13 is beyond anything mankind usually experiences or expresses. There is a divine quality that shines through, a quality which rings true to conscience and condemns us. We cannot quarrel with the standard Paul sets. We know that true love ought to be precisely what he depicts, but at the same time we hang our heads in shameful admission that such love is beyond us.

> Those words, "I love you," have the power to wonderfully transform both the person who speaks them and the one to whom they are spoken.

Nevertheless, we also know that somehow we were made for that very kind of love and that our failure to experience it is a defect for which we are responsible and for lack of which we feel a deep loss.

Paul is depicting a love that is not of this world. It is additional evidence, as C.S. Lewis points out, that we were made for another world. We recognize it for what real love ought to be, and it strikes a chord in us like the description of a land we have never seen but to which we somehow feel we belong. We need read no other part of the Bible than this "love chapter" to know that man is a fallen creature. We can say "I love you!" and perhaps not even realize that deep inside we really mean "I love me and I want you!" Such is the tragedy of present human experience.

Nevertheless, those words, "I love you," have the power to wonderfully transform both the person who speaks them and the one to whom they are spoken. They are the highest expression of which man is capable as a creature made in the image of God. Some people find these words difficult to speak, and other people find them embarrassing to hear. What we all find nearly impossible to believe is that the God who created the universe has spoken these wonderful words personally and intimately to each of us. And He has done it in a way that no one else could: by entering into our humanity and dying for our sins upon the cross. He has thus so fully proved His love that there is no excuse for ever doubting it.

It is this unparalleled manifestation of God's love that makes Christianity what it is. Many facets of our life in Christ make it unique. Among the most wonderful distinctives is the relationship that each Christian is intended to enjoy with Christ Himself—an intimate, *personal* relationship that is not only unmatched by any of the world's religions but is absolutely essential if someone is to be a Christian.

In contrast, for a Buddhist to have a personal relationship with Buddha is neither possible nor necessary. Neither is the practice of Islam impaired because Muhammad is in the grave. It is no hindrance at all to any of the world's historic religions that their founders are dead and gone. Not so with Christianity. If Jesus Christ were not alive today there would be no Christian faith because He *is* all that it offers. Christianity is not a mass *religion* but a personal *relationship*.

At the heart of this relationship is a fact so astonishing that most Christians, including those who have known the Lord for many years, seldom live in its full enjoyment. It is not that we do not believe it intellectually, but that we find it too wonderful to accept its full implications into our moment-by-moment experience of daily life.

We are like a homely, small-town girl from a very poor family who is being wooed by the handsomest, wealthiest, most powerful, most intelligent, and in every way most desirable man who ever lived. She enjoys the things he gives her, but is not able fully to give herself to him and really get to know him because she finds it too much to believe that *he*, given the choice of all the far more attractive women in the world, really loves *her*. And to leave the familiar surroundings of her childhood—the friends and family that have been all she has known and loved—to go off with this one who seems to love her so much and to become a part of another world so foreign and even inconceivable to her, it is all too overwhelming.

Some of us grew up as children singing "Jesus loves me, this I know, for the Bible tells me so," and found a certain amount of childish comfort in its simple assurance at the time. We never matured in that love, however, because we were not taught to do so. Meanwhile, other loves entered our lives and were given priority over the love of God. In his classic, *The City of God*, Augustine declares that man has become earthly minded and lost his heavenly vision because of a "wrong order of loves"—self has replaced God:

> These two cities were made by two loves: the
> earthly city by the love of self unto the contempt of

God, and the heavenly city by the love of God
unto the contempt of self.

To be sure, we still read the love chapter (1 Corinthians
13) now and then and sing lustily (and at times even with
great feeling) such classics as "The love of God is greater far
than tongue or pen can ever tell...." But we are no longer
children, and the simple fact that "Jesus loves *me*" has
somehow lost its power for us. Not because it is intellectually
too shallow, but because its deeper implications, which we
now begin dimly to perceive, are spiritually and emotionally
too wonderful.

Like the small-town girl, each of us finds it very difficult
to believe that Jesus really loves us. While we appreciate His
blessings, we find it difficult to become intimate with our
heavenly Suitor, because it seems so inappropriate that the
Lord of the universe should be wooing *us*. That He loves
everyone and that we are included in that great love is intellectually accepted, but that He has singled *me* out personally
as an object of that love is too marvelous. My response falls
far short of the joy that He intends for me.

Thus the essence of the Christian life—its true source of
joy and confidence and power—is missing in so much that
calls itself Christian. Many preachers attempt to entice the
world to "come to Christ" with the popular offers of health,
prosperity, an improved society, and long life upon earth,
when the real essence of salvation is to know God and to be
partakers of His love and life.

Man's problem is not that he was driven from an earthly
paradise, but that he was separated from God's presence.
That is the great tragedy. What God lovingly offers is
Himself, a restoration to His presence; no longer in an
earthly garden, but in His heavenly home. "Ye shall seek *me*
and find *me* when ye shall search for *me* with all your heart"
(Jeremiah 29:13) is His promise.

What do we want from the person whom we love? Not
things, not gifts, but closer communion, more love, more

intimate fellowship. Thus it is that we are moved to give *ourselves* in our desire to please the One whom we now love with a passion. We are told that God will give us crowns and rewards in heaven. It is not possible for us to understand what that means because we have such a dim perception of what heaven will be like. Whatever the rewards may be, however, we know that each is an expression of His approval, a declaration that we have in some small way, as He has given the grace, pleased Him. Knowing that fact alone is all the reward we could ever desire and will give us joy for eternity. Its anticipation should give us great joy here and now.

At times in our lives it seems impossible to believe (knowing there is no reason in us for Him to love us) that He could ever be pleased with us. We long to hear His "Well done, good and faithful servant...enter thou into the joy of thy lord" (Matthew 25:23), but fear that it could never be so. Such humility of soul, because it reflects the simple truth of our situation except for His grace, is becoming of a Christian—but at such times we do well to remember the amazing and comforting statement of Scripture:

> Therefore judge nothing before the time, until the Lord come, who both will bring to light the hidden things of darkness and will manifest the counsels of the hearts; *and then shall every man have praise of God* (1 Corinthians 4:5).

Would not such praise give us cause to be pleased with ourselves and thus to imagine that there was something of value in us after all? No. Rather than being pleased with ourselves, we will be overcome with joy that we have pleased the One we love with all our hearts, minds, and strength. Self has been crucified with Christ and He has become our all.

Such will be the wonder of heaven. That He should be pleased with us will bring joy beyond the possibility of present comprehension. That every man will receive praise of God does not mean that each will be praised in the same way or to the same degree. Every cup will overflow with joy, but some cups will no doubt be deeper than others. There will be no need for us to recognize such differences, however, were they even apparent, for such comparisons would be meaningless in heaven's bliss. All that He is, the full infinitude of His person, will be equally available to all.

David, who knew the Lord very well, tells us the secret of that intimate relationship which he enjoyed: "One thing have I desired of the LORD, that will I seek after; that I may dwell in the house of the LORD all the days of my life, to behold the beauty of the LORD, and to enquire in his temple" (Psalm 27:4). There can be no doubt that knowing God and experiencing the wonder of His love was the continual and intense longing of David's heart, as so many of his psalms attest: "O God, thou art my God; early will I seek thee: my soul thirsteth for thee…" is the way Psalm 63 begins, and this same passion is expressed in so many others.

In spite of the rejection he experienced by family and friends during so much of his life, David's heart was filled with the joy of the Lord—a joy that strengthened him for the many trials he endured. He also had a deep understanding of heaven and knew that the joy he experienced in part during this brief life of faith would be realized in its fullness there. It is the anticipation of the heavenly joy and, yes, intense *pleasure* of God's presence, that raises our hopes from this earth to heaven. In another psalm, David had written:

> Thou wilt show me the path of life; in thy presence is fullness of joy; at thy right hand there are pleasures forevermore (Psalm 16:11).

Paul indicated that in the last days men would be "lovers of pleasures more than lovers of God" (2 Timothy 3:4). What an indictment. How it challenges us to reexamine our priorities. How ashamed we will be one day that the pitiful pleasures of this world could ever have blinded us to the infinite and eternal pleasures God has "prepared for them that love him" (1 Corinthians 2:9). What a bad bargain to exchange the heavenly for the earthly. Writing more than 200 years ago, in *The Power of the Spirit* William Law put it in sharp perspective:

> And when the lusts of the flesh have had their last day, and the pride of life has only a dead body to inhabit, the soul of man which remains will know at last that it has nothing of its own, nothing that can say, "I do this," or "I possess that."
>
> Then all that man has or does, will either be the glory of God manifested in him, or the power of hell in full possession of his soul. The time of man's playing with words and intellect, of grasping after positions among men or of amusing himself with the foolish toys of this vain world, can last no longer than he is able to eat and drink with the creatures of this world.

"If in this life only we have hope in Christ," declared Paul, "we are of all men most miserable" (1 Corinthians 15:19). The joyful Christian has put his hope in heaven. He is not living for this world and makes sacrifices in this life to please his Lord and to be assured of hearing His "well done" in heaven.

Such is the message of Hebrews 11, where we are given a list of some of the heroes and heroines of the faith and are told of their exploits. The outstanding characteristic of everyone on that roll of honor was the fact that their ultimate hope was in heaven. Confronted by a choice between this world and the one to come, they chose the latter.

God is no man's debtor. The idea that many people have of suffering for Christ and missing out on so much in order to please God is a caricature concocted by Satan. It is certain that no one, when it comes time to die, regrets having missed out on worldly pleasures or treasures or honors as a result of serving God. And how can even those who have lost position and possessions, have been tortured, imprisoned, or killed because of their faith hold any regret that an eternal reward awaits them? Paul reminds us:

> For I reckon that the sufferings of this present time are not worthy to be compared with the glory which shall be revealed in us...For our light affliction, which is but for a moment, worketh for us a far more exceeding and eternal weight of glory (Romans 8:18; 2 Corinthians 4:17).

We know that as His bride we ought to long to be with Christ, and we are sorry that we don't love His appearing as we should. How can we reawaken our love for Him? First of all, we need to remember that love is not merely a sentiment that sweeps over us and which is beyond our control. Marriages are breaking up among Christians because husband or wife claims no longer to love the other and often has "fallen in love" with someone else. This is not love at all, but a Hollywood-inspired counterfeit.

Love involves unshakable *commitment* of oneself to another—thus it involves not just emotions but an act of the *will*. Christ is our example, and husbands are to love their wives as He loved the church. A Christ-like marriage, as C.S. Lewis points out, would not be all peaches and cream, but may well involve suffering hatred and abuse and misunderstanding while giving love in return. That is what Christ did, and that is the kind of love husbands are to have for their wives.

Not only does love require a faithful commitment, but it is a commitment in response to God's command: "Thou shalt love the Lord thy God with all thy heart, and with all thy soul, and with all thy strength, and with all thy mind; and thy neighbor as thyself" (Luke 10:27). Love does indeed involve deep emotion, but it is first of all obedience to God's command. We can love our husband or wife or parent or mother-in-law and even our enemy, no matter how much evil we think they have done to us. It simply takes the willingness to let God pour out His love through us.

Christ has committed Himself to us for eternity, and He expects us to make the same commitment to Him. And that commitment involves loving others if we truly love Him—for a lack of love for our brother is, according to Scripture, proof that we do not really love God (1 John 4:20,21). How much more is the insistence that we cannot love wife or husband or parent a betrayal of the fact that our love for God, no matter how loudly we profess it, is not genuine at all.

There is another motive for loving Christ's appearing. It is not only that we long to see Him for ourselves, but we also want to see Him glorified on this earth where He has been rejected for so long. What a tragedy that "He was in the world, and the world was made by him, and the world knew him not" (John 1:10). The hearts of those who love Christ are grieved that this world, blinded by pride, goes about its business building its plastic utopia in complete disregard for the One who longs to rescue it from an eternity of horror which it is bringing upon itself.

If we love our Lord, then we will want to see Him revealed to the world and made known for who He is. We want to see Him honored and praised where He was rejected. We long to see Him rule, whose right it is to rule, and we want to be at His side, singing His praises, pointing men to Him who is the Lover of our souls.

Our relationship with Christ and with God through Him will forever be one of perfect love. When we see Him, faith and hope will have given place to sight. But love, the greatest gift of all, will endure forever.

Other books by
Dave Hunt

Beyond Seduction

A Cup of Trembling

Death of a Guru

Global Peace and the Rise of Antichrist

The God Makers

How Close Are We?

In Defense of the Faith

The New Spirituality

Occult Invasion

The Seduction of Christianity

A Woman Rides the Beast